HE IS WORTHY

Charles F. Keen

FirstBible International
3148 Franklin Road
Murfreesboro, TN 37128
615-796-0043

Copyright 2005 by Charles F. Keen. All rights reserved.

ISBN 1-933594-23-3

DEDICATION

This book is dedicated to Dr. Ralph McCoy, sometimes referred to as "McCoy of the Mountains." He and his wife raised five dedicated children on the mission field. They also spent much of their lives in the mountains of Mexico where they started the famed Bethesda Homes for tribal children. These homes became a primary tool in their ministries of church planting and tribal evangelism. He also founded Mt. Abarim Baptist Mission International, which has continued to grow into a world-wide ministry even after his home going in 1996.

I first met Dr. McCoy in 1967 during a trip into Mexico. I was twenty-seven years old and had been pastoring in Milford, Ohio for three years. Though missions was not in my background nor part of my ministry philosophy, meeting him changed all that. He took me into his mountains to visit villages, some by plane and others like Tepeyac and Tlapa by riding on donkeys. Little did I know this first trip would create in me a love affair with the whole world. I have now visited almost every continent and dozens of countries all because of a quiet man who lived in the mountains of Mexico. His influence on my life is incalculable. Either knowingly or unknowingly, my trip to Dr. McCoy's still plays into my daily philosophy of ministry and missions.

FOREWORD

Dr. Charles Keen, one of American fundamentalism's foremost missionary spokesmen, has written a remarkable treatise on reaching the unreached in his book entitled <u>HE IS WORTHY</u>. Like an attorney, he builds a case for evangelizing the world with emphasis on the millions who have never heard the name of Jesus nor been told of His love and sacrifice for them. Dr. Keen makes it clear that the motive for winning the lost is one's love for Christ, not simply a love for souls.

Dr. Keen's insight into God's program of reaching the unreached qualifies him to write about the means and methods set forth in Scripture to propagate the gospel in the regions beyond where there are no churches, no Bibles, and no missionaries.

Reading this book has given me a more clearly defined outlook on missions and intensified my burden for the twelve thousand people groups who need Christ. Every page pulsates with Dr. Keen's heartbeat for the more than half of the world's population who remain unreached. He pours his soul into the book enabling the reader to garner from his compassionate spirit a genuine concern for the cause dearest to God's heart. Missions must go beyond the countries where missionaries are already established to *"every kindred, and tongue, and people, and nation"* (Revelation 5:9). This is what Dr. Keen sees as the mission of the church.

<u>HE IS WORTHY</u> is a must for every pastor and Christian. It is sure to be on the best-selling list of Christian books across America. Reading this book will bring a new dimension and new horizons for those who are genuinely concerned for missions around the world to every creature. It should be required reading for every missions major in every Bible college in our country.

— **Raymond W. Barber**

PREFACE

The title of this book, <u>HE IS WORTHY</u>, reduces the author's missions philosophy to a three word phrase. He believes we need to write the triune Godhead back into our mission efforts. God's desire to be worshipped by some from every tribe, nation, people and tongue is the motive for world evangelism, not the eternal welfare of man. Man will profit because we do mission work, but man's eternal welfare is not sufficient motivation to propel and sustain our involvement.

It takes four churches to produce one missionary. One-half of our missionaries do not return for a second term. The author contends that the reason for this low recruitment and low retention rate is largely due to our low motivation factor.

Nothing but a love for God is sufficient to motivate the church and its membership to pay the price world evangelism requires. A love for sinners and a burden for the lost lack sufficiency. It is lack of a scriptural basis.

Paul, the model, performed his ministry, not out of a humanistic approach, but for *"the glory of God."* He also said *"the love of Christ constraineth us,"* not the love for souls. In Romans 15:9 he said, *"... that the Gentiles might glorify God ... for this cause I will confess to thee among the Gentiles..."* The "cause" is that which He asked Peter in John 21, *"... lovest thou me more than these?"* Again, the issue is not our love for the lambs, but the Lord; not our love for the sheep, but the Shepherd; not our love for sinners, but the Saviour. Paul said, *"Do all to the glory of God."*

He is worthy! He desires to be glorified and has developed a plan that includes the church's assignment to bring it about. Let us write God back into our world evangelism. He is worthy!

TABLE OF CONTENTS

HE IS WORTHY	11
THE GLOBALLY SIGNIFICANT CHURCH	23
THE CAUSE	35
THE UNREACHED	47
THE EXPECTATION	57
YOUR PURPOSE	69
YOUR PART IN HIS PROGRAM	79
GETTING ON THE SAME PAGE	93
GOD WANTS YOU TO BE GOOD AT GIVING	103
ON PREACHING	113
WHAT I WISH I HAD KNOWN	123
DEFINITIONS	133
TOP 100 UNREACHED PEOPLE GROUPS	134
COUNTRIES IN THE 10/40 WINDOW	136

HE IS WORTHY

"And he said, Who art thou, Lord? And the Lord said, I am Jesus whom thou persecutest: it is hard for thee to kick against the pricks. And he trembling and astonished said, Lord, what wilt thou have me do? And the Lord said unto him, Arise, and go into the city, and it shall be told thee what thou must do."

Acts 9:5-6

In my opinion, this is the account of Christianity's greatest product, Paul. Christianity is the product of Christ and His life and teachings, and Paul is the product of that Christianity. He was a missionary.

What is the real issue we are dealing with in any service to Christ and especially in world evangelism? Some would think it is the need of others, and that is an issue. Missionaries try to show church members, through slides and displays, that the world is a needy place. Another issue is your ability to participate, and we challenge you to have a meaningful part, to address the need, to give by faith.

Neither the need nor our ability is the main issue. Rather, it is this question: "Is He worthy?" For us to have a meaningful part in world evangelism, we will have some demands put upon us. We have to ask ourselves if He is worthy of these demands. Is He worthy of what it will cost me to serve Him?

He has put monetary demands upon many of you. You have to ask yourself if He is worthy of the money you are giving. He will ask some of you for your children, as He has asked for two of mine and ten of my grandchildren. My wife and I must ask ourselves if He is worthy of such a demand upon parents and grandparents. He will ask some of you to give up your job or country. Is He worthy of all that? Is He worth me leaving my comfort zone and country, or me giving up family and finances so He can have His way?

That is what Paul had to deal with. He gave his testimony three different times in the book of Acts. The first time was Acts 9:1-10. The next time was Acts 22:6-10. Then he gave it again in Acts 26:12-18. In all three accounts, Paul asked the same two questions in the same order.

The first question is in Acts 9:5. *"Who art thou, Lord?"* With this question he is determining Jesus' worth. Then he asked, in verse 6, *"What wilt thou have me to do?"* With this question he is determining Jesus' will. Too often, you come to church and we challenge you with the **what** question before we challenge you with the **who** question. The real issue is who is asking, not what is being asked. Your response would be more positive if you would have to face who He is before facing what is being asked.

In the New Testament, Jesus never calls people to a place until He first calls them to Himself. We should not wait for the place to be defined before we surrender to the Person. We should go ahead and surrender to Christ and trust Him to put us where He wants us (even when we don't know where that is) because He is worthy. See Abraham's surrender, *"... he went out, not knowing whither he went."*

First question: *"Who art thou, Lord?"*

"I am Jesus."

Second question: *"What wilt thou have me to do?"*

I see that same principle throughout the Word of God. The first thing the devil did to entice Adam and Eve to sin was reduce the worthiness of God in their eyes. The devil came to Eve in Genesis 3:1 and said, *"Yea, hath God said, Ye shall not eat of every tree of the garden?"* What he was telling her was this: "God is making unrealistic demands on you." He tried to demote God in Eve's eyes.

In verse 4 he demoted God again in Eve's eyes by challenging His honesty or character. *" ... Ye shall not surely die."*

In verse 5 he told Eve that God was trying to keep the good life from her and Adam. *"For God doeth know that in the day ye eat thereof, then your eyes shall be opened, and you shall be as gods, knowing good and evil."* Satan told Eve this after God had instructed her that she would die if she ate of it (Genesis 2:17 and 3:3).

He was reducing the worth of God in the eyes of Adam and Eve, and the net result was that they sinned. If we do not have a high opinion of the God of Heaven, we will not do right. Do not let the devil do to you what he did to Adam and Eve. He tried to get Eve to reduce God's worth. She did, which led to their sin.

I believe there is a recognizable thread running through Scripture that supports our theme of answering the **who** question before dealing with the **what** question.

Consider the example of MOSES. In Exodus 3 we find the famous story of Moses at the burning bush. God came to Moses there, and in verse 4, he received "the call" from God. Look at verse 6: *"Moreover he said, I am the God of thy father, the God of Abraham, the God of Isaac, and the God of Jacob."* He was establishing His worth in Moses' mind.

Then Moses said, "If I go, who will I say sent me?" God answered, "Tell them I AM sent you." That was all Moses needed. After he established God's worth, he was willingly obedient to God's will. He went to Egypt, out of his comfort zone, performed miracles as God instructed him, and delivered a million people out of the hand of Pharoah. Going into a far country to deliver people from the oppression of Satan sounds like missions to me.

Moses did all of that after God's worth was established in his heart. If we are going to do what we should do as Christians, the first thing we must decide is that He is worthy. God is working in your life today so you will give, or go, or pray. You will never do that to the fullest until you realize that He is worthy.

Consider the example of ISAIAH. We all know the story of Isaiah. He is the most famous missionary in the Old Testament, the one who said in Isaiah 6:8, *"Here am I; send me."* He was a volunteer. But do you know what took place before he said that? He said in Isaiah 6:1, *"I saw the Lord sitting upon a throne, high and lifted up, and his train filled the temple."* He saw the Lord on His throne, and He was worthy in his eyes. When he saw the worthiness of the Lord, he said, "He's worth it. I'll go."

The bottom line is that God is worthy of whatever demands He is putting on you. Until we see that He is worthy, we will not do His will to the degree that we should and have a meaningful impact in world evangelism.

Consider the example of the WISE MEN. There is much we know about the wise men of Jesus' birth, but there is also much we do not know. It seems that Hallmark knows more about them than we do. We do not know how many there were (Hallmark says three), or from where they came. But we do know that they determined the worth of Jesus <u>before</u> they settled on how much they would give.

They said, "We have seen and have come to worship." Then they presented their gifts. Look at the progression. They saw the star; they came to worship the Saviour; then they gave their silver. If we are going to give as we should, it will be because we decided that He is worthy of what He is demanding from us.

The wise men were the first Gentile givers (law of first mention) recorded in the New Testament. Their giving was **planned**, which is the way ours should be. It was **protected** so that someone else would not get it. It was **published** so that we know today what they gave (that is not something most of us would be too excited about in our own giving). It was **proxy** giving; they gave it to His family, which represents the church for us. It was **purposeful** giving. Why did they give? What was the result? It was to get Jesus farther than He had been up to that point. He was born in Bethlehem, He made it to Jerusalem, then after receiving their gift, His family went to Egypt.

That sounds like missions to me. More than three billion people have not yet seen the lowly Lord nor heard the message of the gospel. Our giving helps us get Christ farther than He had been before we gave.

The wise men also had total **participation** in giving. Everyone had a part. Would it be wonderful if everyone in your church gave something, and everyone gave more than they did last year? More is needed because there is still more to do, more that can be done, more of you, and less time.

The real issue in missions is His worth. Jesus thought He was worthy enough that He came out of His grave and immediately gave the Great Commission. In Matthew 28, He said, *"All power is given unto me in heaven and in earth. Go ye therefore ... "* He said that in His freshly resurrected state.

Consider the example of the APOSTLES. Think about this. Jesus gave that challenge to a small group, maybe as small as 11, and urged them to take on the world of 900 million as their responsibility. A single church against the whole world. In accepting that, 10 of the 11 remaining disciples became martyrs. We need to ask ourselves what we will give in obedience to Him, and if He is worth it. The key is in the fact that they saw Him and said, *"Thou are the Christ, the Son of the living God."* Put another way, "Thou art worthy."

Consider the example of DAVID. David thought the Lord was worth it, so in I Samuel 17 he said, "I know fighting Goliath is a big challenge, far bigger than I am. But He is worth it." God was too great to be defied by the armies of the Philistines. So he went, and in his victory exalted his God above the gods of the Philistines, as recorded in verse 46, *" ... that all the earth may know that there is a God in Israel."* It worked because we are still talking about it half a world away and three thousand years later.

Consider the example of the THREE HEBREW CHILDREN. Shadrach, Meshach and Abednego thought He was worth it. In Daniel 3 they said, "We are not going to bow down to another king. The Lord is our God, and He will keep us safe in the furnace. But even if He doesn't, we will do what is right." They were letting the world know that they thought He was worth it.

Consider the example of DANIEL. Daniel thought He was worth it. In Daniel 6 they said they would put him in the lions' den if he kept praying to the Lord, but Daniel bowed toward Jerusalem three times a day knowing the danger. What else could he do — because he considered Him worth it.

HE IS WORTHY

<u>We all need to realize that Jesus Christ is worthy.</u> Most of us preachers probably should just preach more about Jesus and less about a lot of other things and issues.

I heard a story about a young couple with a baby. It was winter, and all of the neighbors came over for refreshments. They stacked their coats on the bed, and after drinking their coffee and visiting for a while, someone said, "Where is the baby?" They discovered that they had smothered the baby with their coats. They never saw the very thing for which they had come. I think that sometimes we have so much going on in our churches that when people come to see Jesus, we never get around to showing Jesus to them. "Show us the Father," Philip said.

Paul thought He was worthy. He said, *"I count all things ... but dung, that I might win Christ."*

The angels think He is worthy. They fly around Heaven, crying, "Holy, holy, holy, Lord God Almighty." The four beasts and the twenty-four elders think He is worthy.

God the Father thought He was worthy. He said in Matthew 3:17, *"This is my beloved Son, in whom I am well pleased."*

All of these people said that Jesus is worthy. What do you say? Is He worthy enough for you to give up what He wants you to give up for His name to get around the world?

There are a couple of things you need to realize right now:

1. He wants to be worshipped by some from every nation, kindred, tribe and tongue. Is He worthy of that worship?

2. If He gets that worship, it is going to cost you something that you are not yet paying. Is He worthy of that?

When my daughter was eight years old, she told my wife and me that she had surrendered her life to be a missionary. No one takes an eight-year-old very seriously, but as she grew up she never forgot that commitment. When she was dating, one of the very first questions she would ask is, "What are you going to do with your life?" If the answer did not include being a missionary, she did not have much time for them because she was going to be a missionary.

When she decided to go to Tennessee Temple University, she told me, "I'm going down there to find a man. All the boys in this church are a bunch of drips." So I said OK. She went down there and married a man from our church. It cost me thousands of dollars for her to find a man that she could have found back home in the pew next to her if she had just looked around.

So for me, the issue was, "Is He worthy of my daughter?" Of course, the answer is yes, and the answer for you should be the same.

A few years later, another of our daughters was married. Her name is Joy. She married the son of a preacher, one of the staff members at the church; they are a fine family. One night she called me and said, "Dad, I want to talk to you. Are you sitting down?"

Just being a smart aleck, I told her, "Tell me anything you want. Just don't tell me you're going to be a missionary."

She said, "Dad, tonight Dan surrendered to go to Africa."

You know, I am just human. I am a father and a grandfather. I said, "God, I've already given you one. Do you want another one from my family?"

I have four children. God told me, "Charles, I gave all I had. I only had one, and I gave Him." I said to my wife, "He's worthy."

You need to decide if He is worthy enough for you to surrender whatever He asks of you. Is He worthy? Well, He gave up Heaven so you could get there. He was rich, but for our sakes he became poor, that you through His poverty might be rich.

We cannot comprehend what it meant for Him to do that. He came down from Heaven, where He was honored and worshipped as God, walked on streets of gold, and lived in mansions. He came down here and became homeless. *"The Son of Man hath not where to lay his head."* He is worthy.

He rode on the clouds, then came here and borrowed a

donkey. He is worthy.

He owned the universe, and when He died, all He had was what was on His back. He is worthy.

He was worshipped in Heaven, and they spit on Him here. He is worthy.

He wore a crown up there, and He wore a crown (of thorns) here, too. He is worthy.

I used to box, and I can have a bit of a short fuse. If you spit on me, I am not responsible for what might happen. The Bible says that they buffeted Jesus, which means that they put a hood over His head and hit Him when He could not see it coming and brace Himself for it.

Do you know what He did on the cross? He took enough for you that God had no judgment left for you. All of God's judgment was poured out on Christ on the cross. He is worthy.

The Bible says that He prayed, *"Let this cup pass from me."* The cup was not the cross. There was something far greater He was about to experience than the nails, the spear, the crown, the cat-o-nine-tails, and the suffocation. For the first time in His eternal existence, He was about to be shunned by the Father.

He had always been in perfect fellowship with the Father, and the Father with Him. He had never done anything to bring any kind of strife or separation between the two of them. But as He hung on the cross, He said, "My God, my God, why hast thou forsaken me? Where are you? Why have you turned your back on me?"

He did that for someone like Charles F. Keen, who was a hellion, did not love God, did not care about Christ, never read the Bible, and never prayed. God, in His love, punished His Son for a guy like me and a person like you. He is worthy.

Then, after saving us, He comes back and says, "I'd like to be worshipped by some from every nation, kindred, tribe and tongue. Would you give so I could be worshipped?"

You need to ask Him today, "Who are you, Lord?" Then ask

Him, "What would you have me do?"

He will say, "I want to put you out of your comfort zone. I want you to give by faith. I want you to give enough so that I can get the glory. I want you to participate so we can have victory."

He might come to some and say, "I want you to become a real prayer warrior." Get a prayer list and start begging God for those people you have never seen and will never see until you get to Heaven. Pray for people in countries whose names you cannot even pronounce, because He is worthy.

He is going to come to some of you parents like He did to me and my wife. From where do missionaries come? They come from churches just like yours and homes like yours. Is He worthy enough to come into your home and take your precious son, and put him in some place where you might see him once every three or four years? Is He worthy enough for you to give your daughter or your grandchildren?

The issue is not money. It is not children. It is this: "Is He worthy?"

He wants worship. If He wants it, I want to do what I can to get it for Him. It is about our love for Him. *"For the love of Christ constraineth us ..."*

A little fourth-grader was in a class of thirty-three plus himself. He was not well-liked; he usually played outside by himself (if he went outside at all). Often he would sit in the doorway. He walked to school and back home by himself. It grieved his mother's heart, but he was just an outcast.

One day he came home and said, "Mother, the teacher said that this Friday is Valentine's Day, and we are supposed to make valentines for everyone in class." He then asked her for supplies to complete that project: scissors, staples, glue, construction paper and a ruler. Her heart sank because she knew he would get none back, but she bought what he needed. He worked diligently that week to make thirty-three valentines.

When Friday morning came, he went off to school with his

HE IS WORTHY

sack of valentines in his hand. His mother made cookies while he was at school and waited to greet him with cookies and milk because she knew he would be sad. He came home, set down his book bag and walked past her. She did not see his face, but he said, "Mom, not one. Not one."

She was crushed. "How will I ever comfort him?" she thought. But she brought the cookies and milk to the table for him, and as he sat down to eat he looked up at her with a big smile.

"Not one," he said again. "I didn't miss one. I made one for everyone in the class."

When I heard that story, I thought how much we as Christians can relate to it. The world is no friend to us. They do not love us; they make laws against us and ostracize us. We are supposed to carry a love story to them, and let them know that they are loved by the God of Heaven, who gave His son, the Lord Jesus, to die on a cross.

One day, you and I will stand before the dear Lord Jesus, whom God gave, and who gave His life. I want to be able to say, "Lord, I wasn't a great preacher, and I wasn't loved by the world. I didn't amount to much as far as the world was concerned. I tried to get the gospel to everyone. I tried to give it to those who had it and those who did not have it. I tried to give it to those on my continent and those on other continents. I tried to give it to those who had a Bible and those who had never seen one." I want to do the best I can so I can say, "Not one, Lord. I didn't miss one."

You might say, "Brother Keen, there's no way you can do that. You're sixty-five years old. You'll never be around long enough to do it." But I can at least say, "Lord, I didn't get there, but I was headed in that direction, and I tried to get a few churches to go with me."

God gave His son. Christ gave His life. Missionaries give. We give our silver, ourselves, and our seed because He is worthy.

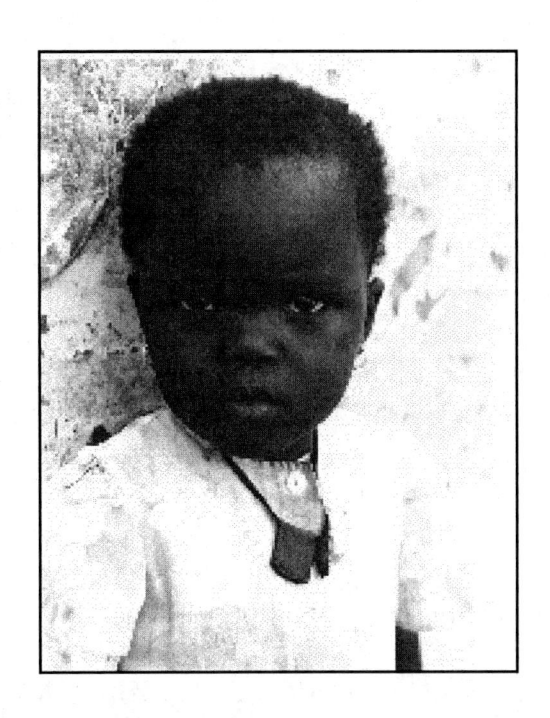

THE GLOBALLY SIGNIFICANT CHURCH

"And it came to pass, that after three days Paul called the chief of the Jews together: and when they were come together, he said unto them, Men and brethren, though I have committed nothing against the people, or customs of our fathers, yet was I delivered prisoner from Jerusalem into the hands of the Romans."
Acts 28:17

"And Paul dwelt two whole years in his own hired house, and received all that came in unto him, Preaching the kingdom of God, and teaching those things which concern the Lord Jesus Christ, with all confidence, no man forbidding him."
Acts 28:30-31

In Acts 28, we find out that Paul goes to Rome. Now there is some discussion about the chronology of Paul's life. Whatever you believe as to the order of Paul's visits to Rome, there is one obvious thing on which we can agree. He saw two things about the Roman church.

1. They wanted to be globally significant.

2. They had some things on which to work if they were going to be globally significant. He observed this during his two years there.

With that in mind, look at Romans 15:18-28. *"For I will not dare to speak of any of those things which Christ hath not wrought by me, to make the Gentiles obedient, by word and deed, Through mighty signs and wonders, by the power of the Spirit of God; so that from Jerusalem, and round about unto Illyricum, I have fully preached the gospel of Christ. Yea, so have I strived to preach the gospel, not where Christ was named, lest I should build upon another man's foundation: But as it is written, To whom he was not spoken of, they shall see: and they that have not heard shall understand. For which cause also I have been much hindered from coming to you. But now having no more place in these parts, and having a great desire these many years to come unto you; Whensoever I take my journey into Spain, I will come to you: for I trust to see you in my journey, and to be brought on my way thitherward by you, if first I be somewhat filled with your company. But now I go unto Jerusalem to minister unto the saints. For it hath pleased them of Macedonia and Achaia to make a certain contribution for the poor saints which are at Jerusalem. It hath pleased them verily; and their debtors they are. For if the Gentiles have been made partakers of their spiritual things, their duty is also to minister unto them in carnal things. When therefore I have performed this, and have sealed to them this fruit, I will come by you into Spain."*

Paul knows the church at Rome wants to be globally significant, so he is going to point out some things on which they need to work, and then he is traveling on to Spain.

Because many of us want our churches to be globally significant, let us look at just what that means.

I. First, there is the **requirement** of a church that wants to be globally significant.

Most of your churches have requirements for your missionaries, and you should. Their age might be important to you. Their education probably has some value. You want to know about their families, their doctrine, their associates, and their health. It is not wrong for you to ask that of missionaries. However, maybe missionaries should have some requirements for you as a church to meet before they decide to sign on with you.

Did it ever dawn on you that there might be some requirements for a church to meet before it signs on with a missionary? I see so many missionaries get questionnaires from churches, so I thought it might be good to send questionnaires to those churches. What is the requirement of a church that genuinely wants to affect the world with the gospel of Jesus Christ?

Some may think that a large mission budget is a requirement. Of course, it is not wrong to have that and it is often needed, but it is not the main requirement. Others may think that you need a growing missions family. I do not want this to sound bad, but a lot of preachers brag about how many missionaries they have. I hope those numbers grow, but that is not the real requirement. It is good to be globally aware and know everything about what is going on in the world. That is not the answer either.

In these chapters in Romans, Paul shows us what we must be if we are to be globally significant as a church. In Romans 15:5, Paul says, *"Now the God of patience and consolation grant you to be likeminded one toward another according to Christ Jesus."* Underline the word <u>likeminded</u>. Why did he bring that up? He wants to show us the <u>requirement for being effective in world evangelism</u>. It is not very exciting, but it is important. It is unity of membership.

Some of you are thinking, "You are making too much of this." Look at verse 6: *"That ye may with one mind and one mouth glorify God, even the Father of our Lord Jesus Christ."*

Now read Romans 16:17. *"Now I beseech you, brethren, mark them which cause divisions and offences contrary to the doctrine which ye have learned; and avoid them."*

Paul decided, after two years of observation, that the Roman church needed to have more unity if it was going to be effective.

Now go to Romans 12:10. *"Be kindly affectioned one to another with brotherly love; in honour preferring one another."*

Verse 16: *"Be of the same mind one toward another. Mind not high things, but condescend to men of low estate. Be not wise in your own conceits."*

Verse 18: *"If it be possible, as much as lieth in you, live peaceably with all men."*

Romans 14:1 says, *"Him that is weak in the faith receive ye, but not to doubtful disputations."*

Verse 4: *"Who art thou that judgest another man's servant? to his own master he standeth or falleth. Yea, he shall be holden up: for God is able to make him stand."*

Verse 10: *"But why dost thou judge thy brother? or why dost thou set at nought thy brother? for we shall all stand before the judgment seat of Christ."*

Verse 13: *"Let us not therefore judge one another any more: but judge this rather, that no man put a stumbling block or an occasion to fall in his brother's way."*

Verse 19: *"Let us therefore follow after the things which make for peace, and things wherewith one may edify another."*

Almost every church in the Bible had a dominant problem which they had to confront. The church at Corinth had to deal with immorality. The church at Ephesus had to deal with losing its first love. The church at Colosse had to deal with gnosticism.

The church at Thessalonica had to deal with confusion over the Second Coming.

The problem with the church at Rome was a lack of unity of membership, and Paul was telling them that if they were to remain effective, they must maintain unity. They could not be fragmented, fractured or splintered. I pastored for 35 years, and I must say to you that the pastor is not the only man in the crowd on patrol. Everyone, from the ladies in the nursery to the men in the parking lot, needs to be deputized to help bring and maintain unity among the brethren. I do not want to come to church and not be able to use the left aisle because a certain person is also using it or we cannot sit on the same side of the auditorium with so-and-so.

There are so many ways to keep unity out of a fundamental Baptist church; we should patent some of them.

"Why did you sing that song? You know that is my song."

"Why did you park in my parking space? I always park there, if I come."

"I always sit there. You know that."

I used to think that we needed unity so it would be fun to go to church. I know now that we need it so that we can work for God as a church.

Now let us consider why Paul thought unity was so important. I can think of two reasons.

1. You need unity to be effective in prayer. I am a missionary, and any missionary will tell you that the greatest contribution you can make is to pray for us. If you give money and not prayer, you are only sending us to defeat, to come back home, and to lose our children. We need your prayers, and you cannot pray effectively for us if you are fighting among yourselves.

Have you ever noticed that the missionary is usually the only full-time Christian worker who gives out a prayer card? I know more pastors than you can imagine, and not one of them has ever given me a prayer card. I had a Christian school when I was a pastor, and I never had a school administrator give me a prayer card. I have never had a singer give me a prayer card. We give them because we know the necessity of it to our survival.

2. You need unity so you can have power. If you think you have trouble now, just decide that you really want to be worldwide in your church's gospel presentation, and the devil will show up like he never had in your lifetime. You can reach your neighborhood and your city, and he might not worry quite as much about you. But you start to send out missionaries, mission dollars, and strive to be effective around the world, and he will move into places you never even knew you had. He will use people you would never suspect.

I have found that most churches are in missions to be respectable, not to bring world evangelism to closure. They approach it the way I would run the Boston Marathon. I am 66 years old and a few pounds overweight. If I entered that race, do you really think I would be doing it to win? I might not show up for days. But I could tell my grandchildren, "Grandpa ran the Boston Marathon." I would be running just so I could say I participated, not to do anything of value. There are many churches that are involved in missions just because they are supposed to be, without any thought of being effective for God.

I recently read a book entitled <u>Tally-Ho the Fox</u>. What a strange title for a book about missions. It said that the title would be explained in Chapter 17, so I went there first.

The author said that in England, where they have fox hunts, a man had a pen full of dogs that laid around, fought with each other over their food and water, chewed on each other, or just slept in the corner. Then the gate was thrown open, the horn was blown, and the dogs heard the command, "Tally-ho the fox!" Suddenly there was a great unity among the dogs and they all had the same goal. They forgot about chewing on each other and started going after the fox.

It should be the same way with us. Jesus has come and given

HE IS WORTHY

the command, "Go into all the world and preach the gospel." We need to have some unity about us and go after that goal. Unity is the requirement for being effective for God and globally significant. As Psalm 133 says, *"Behold, how good and how pleasant it is for brethren to dwell together in unity!"*

II. There is the **reason** we should want to be globally significant — Romans 15:9. *"And that the Gentiles might glorify God for his mercy; as it is written, For this cause I will confess to thee among the Gentiles, and sing unto thy name."* It is repeated in verses 10-12.

We have humanized our approach to missions. We are into visualization. I know that the eye affects the heart, and there is value in visual aids, but only a fire for God and a broken heart for souls will cause people to respond the way they should. It will never work as long as we keep the human destiny of others as our primary goal. We must have God as the reason we do what we do.

Paul said in Romans 15:9, *"... that the Gentiles might glorify God ..."* "For the glory of God, for this cause; this is why I am a missionary." He also said, "The love of Christ constrains us." Jesus said, *"Simon, lovest thou me more than these ... feed my sheep."* Until we see that it is for God's glory, we will not give our silver, ourselves, or our seed. The first and most consuming reason for missions has to be for the glory of God and not just about man. Until we get that established in our hearts, we will not be able to do the job we need to do.

I have a daughter and son-in-law on the mission field, first in Australia and now in South Africa. I had another daughter and her husband to surrender and go to Africa. When my second daughter told me their decision, my first reaction was, "That's not fair. Some people haven't given any and now I'm giving two children and ten grandkids."

Then God said, "Am I worth it?"

And I said, "Yes, Lord, but I'm human. I'll give them up for you, though."

I have seen my wife walk the hallway in our former home, where pictures were hung of all our kids, and stand there and weep. If He is not the reason, this is a lousy way to get through life. I do not love people enough, but I do love Him enough.

III. Look at the **reach** of those who want to be globally significant. Romans 15:19 says, *"Through mighty signs and wonders, by the power of the Spirit of God; so that from Jerusalem, and round about unto Illyricum, I have fully preached the gospel of Christ."* In this passage, Illyricum is present-day Yugoslavia.

Here is what Paul is saying. He has preached from Jerusalem, in the southeast corner of the Roman Empire, all the way to Illyricum, in the northeast corner. As he says in verse 23, there are no more places for him to preach, *"... now having no more place in these parts,"* where the gospel has not been preached. He did not mean every door had been knocked upon and every man witnessed to, but that through church planting, every home in that area was within reach of the gospel.

So in verse 24 and beyond, he talked about his plans. *"I take my journey into Spain,"* which was the next province beyond Illyricum. He describes Spain at that time in verse 21: *"But as it is written, To whom he was not spoken of, they shall see: and they that have not heard shall understand."* It is the uttermost; it is an unreached people group. He is going where the gospel has not yet been.

You might be wondering, "Does this mean we should quit Mexico and Brazil and Europe and all of the other places we've been reaching all these years?" No. Jerusalem, Judea and Samaria are still part of the Great Commission. But if that is all we are doing, it is not enough. We must realize that we also have a responsibility to the uttermost, "Spain," if you please. That is what Paul was doing here. He said, "I know of a place where there is no gospel yet."

You have probably heard of the 10/40 Window. There are 66

nations in that area, from 10 degrees north latitude to 40 degrees north latitude, stretching from North Africa to Japan. Ninety-seven percent of the people in the world who have not heard the gospel live there. Why won't someone go there? Paul never lost his burden for Israel. But he knew he had to go to Spain.

Part of my burden is to challenge people about their responsibilities concerning the 6,000 languages that still need the Bible. There are 186,000 missionaries, who call themselves Protestant, coming out of the United States. Only 9,000 of those are cross-cultural, church-planting missionaries. There are 85 countries where our kind of fundamentalists do not have a single missionary. By comparison, Avon has 4 million women in 100 countries selling "repair kits." Mary Kay has 450,000 women in America selling their products. God help us.

We give only two-tenths of one percent of our mission dollar to the unreached? More than 99 percent goes from Jerusalem to Illyricum. Meanwhile, there are 6,000 unreached people groups in the world. That sounds like a big job, but for every one of those groups there are 600 local congregations. It was a much bigger job for the New Testament church in Jerusalem. When they got the Great Commission, there was one church for 900 million people on Earth, and every country was closed.

"But Brother Keen, all of those churches today are not like us." That is true. But while there are 6,000 unreached people groups, there are also 12,000 fundamental, independent Baptist churches in the United States alone. There are 12,000 "like us." If every one of those churches adopted one group, we could evangelize the world for God in our generation.

<u>IV. Finally, the **results** of those who will be globally significant.</u> Look at Romans 16:1-24. There are twenty-four families and/or individuals mentioned there. Those are the results of Paul's mission's efforts in Rome, of gospel preaching, of soul-winning, and knocking on doors.

In Romans 1:16, Paul said, *"For I am not ashamed of the*

gospel of Christ: for it is the power of God unto salvation to every one that believeth." He came to Rome thinking, "I know you are a powerful city. You have economic power, social power, military power, intellectual power, but you are a bunch of idolaters, adulterers, homosexuals, and full of all other kinds of wickedness." So he went throughout Rome preaching the gospel, and he proved that it works. On the back side of his letter to the Romans, he named twenty-four of his converts. Wherever you plant the gospel, it will work.

In the fall of 1958, my wife and I went for two months to Akron Baptist Temple wanting to be saved. I had gone there as a boy. They knew me and thought I was already saved, even though I knew I was not. The gospel worked there, and we got saved.

I was preaching recently in Kentucky and saw a man who had a flat nose and a spider web tattooed on his face from his collar all the way up into his hairline. He was the meanest-looking guy. I tried to warm up to him. You know how most of us are, afraid of sinners or of anybody who might be a little different. I was talking to him, and my wife said, "You're staring." I said, "No, I'm studying."

I preached until my heart was sore, thinking all along, "Lord, save that man." He did not get saved. I asked the pastor what this man's story was.

The pastor said his son was out soul-winning, and when he knocked on a door. He heard someone yell, "Come in." He went in and found himself staring down the barrel of a gun.

The man asked, "What are you doing here?" The pastor's son said, "I've come to tell you about Jesus."

The man said, "What about Him?" So the pastor's son gave him the gospel. When he finished, the man said, "You had better believe what you just told me for I'm about to shoot you."

That twenty-year-old son of a pastor said, "I don't want to die, but Jesus died for sinners, and if I die today, I know I am

HE IS WORTHY

saved."

The man put his gun down and said, "Anybody who would believe that at a time like this, it must be real." The pastor's son led him to Christ.

After the man got saved, he said, "I am a convicted rapist waiting for my sentence. I go to prison in two weeks. Do you think I could come to church between now and then?" The pastor's son said, "Sure." So he came to make a public profession of faith. He asked his brother-in-law to come see him get baptized. The man with the spider web tattoo was his brother-in-law.

When I preached, he raised his hand but did not get saved. Two weeks later, the pastor called me and said, "Guess what? Spiderman got saved." The gospel works in Kentucky.

I have been in Africa, Asia, Europe, South America, but I have never been anywhere that I did not see the gospel work. God help us if we know it will work in the regions beyond but we do not send anyone, or any money, or any prayers. We know the people are there, but we try to act like we are not responsible. God loves them, they were made in His image, and His blood will cleanse them.

We are commanded to go into the world and preach the gospel; we know it brings results if we do the requirements, and do the "reach" for the right reason.

THE CAUSE

"And David said, What have I now done? Is there not a cause?"

I Samuel 17:29

We all know this story. We all know the odds were against the winner. We know the outcome. So no one gets nervous when they read it. When David takes off against Goliath, we already know who is going to fall.

I have heard a lot of sermons about the phrase, "Is there not a cause?" But I have never heard anybody talk about the cause.

What was the cause? What motivated David to accept the challenge, and why did no one else accept the challenge? David accepted it because he had a missionary heart.

The cause for which David was fighting is shown in I Samuel 17:10, in which Goliath said, *"I defy the armies of Israel this day."* The Philistines were defying Israel. In verse 25, the men of Israel said of Goliath, *"Surely to defy Israel is he come up."*

Look at verses 45 and 46: *"Then said David to the Philistine, Thou comest to me with a sword, and with a spear, and with a shield: but I come to thee in the name of the LORD of hosts, the God of the armies of Israel, whom thou hast defied. This day will the LORD deliver thee into mine hand; and I will smite thee, and take thine head from thee; and I will give the carcases of the host of the Philistines this day unto the fowls of the air, and to the wild beasts of the earth ... "*

Now here is the cause: *" ... that all the earth may know that there is a God in Israel."*

David's God was being defamed and he was not going to stand for it. He said, "I want to stand up for my God so that all the world may know." It must have worked, because we are talking about what he did half a world away and 3,000 years later.

This is a familiar story. <u>The problem with familiarity is that it robs us of research.</u> Because the story is so exciting, we get caught up in it and it robs us of closely examining the details.

We run with David; we swing our arm as he swings his stone; we hear Goliath fall; we stand by David as he cuts off the head of the giant. We stand with him as he stands before the king

HE IS WORTHY

with the sword and the head of the defeated in his hand. Good triumphs over evil. We all know that, and it is wonderful. But there is something deeper than that.

Goliath is nine feet, six inches tall. He is a warrior, with a big helmet, a big spear and a big shield. He has an armor bearer who goes before him. He is a big enemy.

<u>But there is a bigger enemy in this story than Goliath, and that enemy is a lack of ability to recruit.</u> As soon as the army of Israel found someone to go in verse 32, the enemy was defeated. So the problem was not out there in the valley. It was at the campfire. The problem today is not out there in the world, but around the pulpit, at the altar and in the pews.

In our story we have two groups of people. We have those who would not accept recruitment; they could not go or did not go. We have one who did accept recruitment, and he did go. Let us look at why some did not go though one did, and we can see a mission application.

The biggest Goliath we have to fight today is world evangelism. Jesus gave us the Great Commission five times in His glorified state, from the time of His resurrection until His ascension. Five times He said, "There's your challenge. The world is your goal and your assignment, and it's a big challenge. I want you to go into all the world and preach the gospel."

May I say unto you that most of us are hanging around the campfire, shining our armor and polishing our boots, or combing our plume. Most of us are dressing right, smelling right, and singing right, but we are not going anywhere. And the world is 70 percent "non-Christian" today, with 3.2 billion people having never heard the gospel. Someone is not taking recruitment efforts personally.

<u>Now look at the army of Israel in this story. Why did some of them not go?</u>

I. The first reason they did not get involved is because **they were already involved.** Look at verse 2 of I Samuel 17: *"And*

Saul and the men of Israel were gathered together, and pitched by the valley of Elah, and set the battle in array against the Philistines." Now underline those final eight words, where they "set the battle in array against the Philistines."

Verse 19: "Now Saul, and they, and all the men of Israel, were in the valley of Elah, fighting with the Philistines."

Verse 21: "For Israel and the Philistines had put the battle in array army against army."

So they did not get involved because they were already busy. They were fighting. They were not inactive. They were in the army. They were dressed right; they were trained; they were discipled; they could march. And they were even willing to enter into some skirmishes.

Were they fighting where the battle was to be won? No. The battle was to be won out there in the valley against Goliath.

We fundamentalists are not lazy. Are you kidding? You have to be healthy to belong to our church. We are not inactive. If you are reading this, you probably are not a couch potato.

We have our conferences, our seminars, our retreats and our camps. We fight our lesser enemies. We have our music straightened out, we have our standards, and we take the right stand on social issues. No one can accuse a fundamental Baptist of being inactive.

But I am not sure we are fighting where the battle is to be won. That battle is world evangelism. We are not going to win what Jesus said to win by always fighting over music, or standards, or areas like that. Those things are right and proper and good, but that is not where the battle is going to be won. Just because you might be involved in those other things, it is not up to you to decide that the real battle is not for you. Do not confuse separation with surrender.

A professor came into a classroom at a Christian college with a jar and thirteen rocks. He put the jar on the desk and put the rocks in it. The jar would not hold any more rocks.

HE IS WORTHY 39

"Is the jar full?" he asked.

"Yes, sir," the class replied.

Without saying a word, he reached under the desk and pulled out a bucket of gravel and poured it into the jar. He jiggled the jar so the gravel would filter down around the rocks. He poured until the gravel reached the top of the jar.

"Is the jar full?"

"Yes, it's full now."

He reached down and got a bucket of sand. He poured it in until it reached the top.

"Is the jar full?"

No one in the class answered, because by this time they knew something was up.

Finally, he produced a bucket of water and poured it into the jar so that it filled every bit of space that was left. Then he stopped.

"Now, the jar is full," the professor said before revealing his point: "Put the big stuff in first."

What we, our churches, need to learn to do is put the big stuff in first. According to Jesus, the big stuff is world evangelism.

II. The second reason the army of Israel did not get involved is because **they spent too much time on enemy assessment**.

All through the story, they kept coming back to the size of the enemy (I Samuel 17:4-7, 25, 32). After all, he was nine-feet-six. He had to duck when he walked under a chandelier. He had large armor and an armor bearer.

Look at verse 25: *"And the men of Israel said, Have ye seen this man that is come up?"* They were assessing the enemy. They were saying, "Have you seen this man? Have you seen the size of our challenge, of our assignment?"

They really studied this. They had the facts down. They spent so much time assessing the enemy and his size that they were afraid (verses 11, 32 and 33). We, like them, have a big challenge today. I will be the first to admit that we have a lot of work to do. I can stand here and tell you truthfully that we have over 6,000 languages without the Word of God. That is a big job, and God bless those of you who are helping in that. To my knowledge, until February of 2005, there were 273 tribes or languages with a whole Bible. Now, thanks to many of you, there are 274 — one more than in 2004. But there are 6,000 to go and FBI is working on several more.

Now that is a big job, but if the size of the job is all we talk about, it does two things: it makes us afraid, and we lose our conviction about whether it should be done. We just say to ourselves and to each other, "Surely He didn't mean for us to do that." And we lose our conviction.

I do not run across many people who feel badly because a job is not done. I could tell you there are 6,000 people groups on this earth without the gospel, without a Bible, without a church, with the doors closed, and I would be telling the truth. That is a big job. I could spend all of my time assessing the enemy, but that is not the whole truth.

It is a big job, but we have a big God, and the battle is His.

Goliath is so big he has to duck when he walks under a chandelier. God is so big He has to duck when He walks under a star. He is so immense that the universe is in Him instead of Him being in the universe. He is omnipotent, omniscient and omnipresent.

The battle is the Lord's. It is not your job, or your pastor's job, or my job. It is the Lord's work; we are just going along to give a report. So do not spend all your time on enemy assessment to the exclusion of your resources. *"And Jesus came and spake unto them, saying, All power is given unto me in heaven and in earth."* (Matthew 28:18)

III. The third reason they did not get involved is because they were victims of **low motivation**. They were not sufficiently motivated to respond to the recruitment challenge.

Look at verse 25: *"... and it shall be, that the man who killeth*

HE IS WORTHY 41

him, the king will enrich him with great riches, and will give him his daughter, and make his father's house free in Israel."

A. Great riches — that was motivation number one. But how many men went out to fight when they heard that? None. They were back in camp shining shoes and polishing armor. Why? Because the prize being offered was not worth the danger that would be incurred in accomplishing the task.

B. So the verse went on to say that whoever succeeded would win the king's daughter. How many went then? None. "Getting her just isn't worth who we have to go up against to get her," they said. This is low motivation.

C. Well, if those enticements would not work, then the king tacked on one more at the end of the verse. Whoever agreed to fight would see his father's house and land become tax-free.

So whoever went to face Goliath would get rich, marry the king's daughter and have his land tax-free (not one "taker").

Now what missionaries have to be careful about is coming into churches in America and giving low motivation. We show some old man on a stump at the headwaters of the Amazon, smoking the peace pipe, shuffling down a path into the dark jungle, and we say, "Give to him." Many of you say, "No."

We tell missionaries to go and evangelize these people. But it takes four churches to produce one missionary because of low motivation — not necessarily because of bad Christians.

We hear, "Give your children; send your kids and tell them to go the jungle and reach that old man for Christ." But most of you would rather have them be a plumber or president. No one is going, but we are still sending money. We are substituting our money instead of going; we are buying our responsibility instead of sending our children.

I have two precious daughters on the mission field. They are beautiful girls. Ten of my grandchildren are over there with them. For my grandson's 13th birthday, as his rite of passage his mother let him get a pocketknife. He was so excited about that pocketknife.

My granddaughter's birthday was last week. She loves animals; I nicknamed her Fido. She is going to be a veterinarian. Since I was going to be in a meeting in Canada during her birthday and would not be able to call her then, I called her a few days early. I told a pastor friend, "You know, it's a dumb way to carry on a grandpa-granddaughter relationship, over a phone or by e-mail." Hugging a phone is just not the same.

I see my wife stand in the hallway and cry as she looks at pictures of our children. They are all over the world, but we are glad to do it. We do not do it for Africans or for Indians. We do it for the God of Heaven.

There is nothing wrong with slides. I have slides, a PowerPoint, and a video. Those are good support tools. But we need a message with a brokenness from our hearts, that these folks need God and He wants to be worshipped by them. For <u>His</u> sake we are going to go, not for <u>their</u> sakes.

So we know why all of the soldiers in Israel did not go. Why did David go? He realized: 1. that the issue was not Goliath, but God; 2. God would be present in the challenge; and 3. past victories were preparation for present challenges.

First, **he realized that the issue was not Goliath, but God**. He said, "You're defying my God, and I'm not going to let the world think that's the kind of God I have." "*... I come to thee in the name of the LORD of hosts, the God of the armies of Israel, whom thou hast defied.*"

Do you know what idolatry is? Idolatry is nothing more than someone's imagination of what your God is. I have been in India, where they have 330 million gods. Some of them are pornographic gods that I would not even describe in male company. They are stone gods, alligators, monkeys, rats and cows.

They look at those and say, "That's God." <u>That's not God</u>! Our God is holy and righteous and just and loving and merciful

HE IS WORTHY

and forgiving and forgetting. How can we stand here and allow half the world to believe that something else is God?

David said, "I'm not going to let those Philistines defile our God or let them think that's the kind of God we have." So he realized that the issue was not Goliath, but God.

There are four reasons for obedience in the Bible. <u>First</u> is obedience out of fear of judgment, and that is not wrong. I do some things because I am afraid I will get in trouble if I do not. <u>Second</u>, there is a desire for a reward, and that is not wrong. The Lord gives out crowns and rewards. The <u>third</u> reason is for the good of others, and that is not wrong. There are things we all do for others. But the <u>fourth</u> and greatest reason for obedience in the Bible is <u>jealousy for God</u>. I am jealous that folks would know the truth about the God who gave His Son for me. I am not going to let them think our God is some kind of grotesque stone-carved image by some deranged witch doctor, or some snake coming out of a wicker basket with a flat head.

David said, "I can't stand for that," and I don't know how you can stand for it. You ought to pray, give and go so they would know the truth about the true and living God.

The second reason David went was because **he realized that God would be present in the challenge.** He said several times, "The battle is the Lord's." He just went along to give the report, to tell what God is doing.

God is here with us today, and not because of you, although He uses people to accomplish His work. We are just giving the report of what God is doing.

Look at verse 49, where David took that sling and hit Goliath right between the eyes. With the rock going toward his head that way, you would think Goliath should have fallen backward, but he fell on his face. I used to box, and I know which way you go when you get hit. I was trained well at it.

Goliath fell on his face because David did not kill him. God killed him. He smacked him right in the back of the head.

The third reason David accepted recruitment was because **he believed past victories were preparation for present challenges.** Saul told him in verse 33, *"Thou art not able to go against this Philistine to fight with him: for thou art but a youth, and he a man of war from his youth."* "You can't go. You're but a youth, and he a man of war from his youth. You'll never make it. It's more than you can handle. You'll never be victorious doing that."

Then David, in verses 33-36, said, "Saul, let me tell you a story. One time I was herding my sheep and a lion came out of the woods. I grabbed that lion by the beard, broke his neck and stacked him along the side of the road. As I was walking back across the road, feeling good about that victory, here came a bear after that same lamb, and I broke that bear in half and stacked him on top of the lion." (Keen James Version)

I may have embellished that a little bit, but you know the story. I think you see my point. David said, "Because of what God has done in my life in the past, I was prepared for this big challenge."

You did not get where you are, and your church did not get where it is, without some victories. I was a pastor for 35 years and I know that people are people; there is a devil and there is a God; there is a kingdom of darkness and a kingdom of light; and there are forces of evil and forces of good. I know that you have been through some bear-and-lion challenges in the past. God gave you victory, and you are here so He can bring you now to the big challenge, so He can say, "I have helped you with your <u>lion</u>, I have helped you with your <u>bear</u>, now go for your <u>Goliath</u>."

Imagine what you and your church could do financially and to influence other churches if you would just go after your Goliath. When David did his thing, they all took off. *"... the men of Israel and of Judah arose, and shouted, and pursued the Philistines ... returned from chasing after the Philistines, and*

HE IS WORTHY

they spolied their tents." They all got recruited. You would be amazed at the influence you could have if you just decided to believe that God has done what He has done for you so you can handle the big things.

The fourth reason David went was because **he was allowed to be creative.** He said, "If we're to be victorious, we're going to have to do it differently than how we've been doing it."

Saul told him, "If you are going to do this, take my armor and my spear and my shield."

David probably thought, "Saul, if that stuff works so well, why are you sitting here?"

When he put all of that on, he looked like a bus kid. He wiggled his head but the helmet did not go anywhere. So he said, "Saul, I appreciate how we've done it in the past, but this challenge is going to require some new creativity. Will you give me the liberty to do it a new way?"

And Saul said, "Go for it, boy."

We have to learn that we are not going to evangelize the half of the world that does not have the gospel if we do it the way we have always done it. Sure, a lot of battles have been won by that armor, but this is a new battle. We are going to have to do it some new ways. We fundamentalists are not big on that, but we had better get big on that.

David said, "Let me take some smooth stones." You know how many stones he took? Five. Do you know why he took five stones?

Some have said it was because Goliath had four brothers, which he did. I do not know if David knew Goliath's gene pool. I also heard that he took five stones because five is the number of grace. I do not know if he knew systematic theology.

You know why took five stones? That is all he could get in his bag. I do not have any verses for that; there are no verses for the other reasons, either. What I do have a verse for is this: He was allowed to do it a different way.

I believe that if you allow for some different strategy, we can reach a world that has not been reached in church history. If we are always to do like we have always done it, we are always going to have what we have always had.

So, would you accept recruitment? I do not necessarily mean for you to go, but I do mean for you to not be afraid of obedience. God does not want everyone to go; He wants everyone to pray, everyone to give, and some to go. Whatever God wants for you, say, "Speak, Lord, thy servant heareth. Here am I, send me."

There was a man in the New Testament who was possessed by devils. After Jesus cast them out, the man wanted to go with Him. But Jesus said, "No, you go back home and tell them what I have done." He wanted him to stay put and tell his family and friends and the people in his community about Him.

Not everyone is supposed to go, but everyone is to pray, and everyone is to give.

THE UNREACHED

"For when the Gentiles, which have not the law, do by nature the things contained in the law, these, having not the law, are a law unto themselves: Which show the work of the law written in their hearts, their conscience also bearing witness, and their thoughts the mean while accusing or else excusing one another;) In the day when God shall judge the secrets of men by Jesus Christ according to my gospel."

Romans 2:14-16

Now it says in verse 14, *"the Gentiles, which have not the law."* We could say, "the Gentiles, which have not the Bible" or "the Gentiles, which have not the church," or "the Gentiles, which have not the gospel." There is a group of people in this world — Gentiles, (as well as some Jews) or non-Jews, like you and me — who have not yet received the Word of God, a church to attend, or the Lord Jesus. I want you to consider for just a moment the Gentiles that have not yet received the law. They are called the "unreached."

The unreached on this planet today number 3.2 billion. That is half of our world's population. In the 10/40 Window, for which I am burdened, there are 66 nations, which represent 97 percent of all the unreached people in the world.

There are 6,000 unreached people groups that have not yet received the law. The average church gives two-tenths of one percent of each mission dollar to the Gentiles, or the unreached, who have not yet received the law. Over 6,000 languages on earth do not have the Word of God; they are unreached. Very few people are praying for them, and fewer are going to reach them.

I wrote a book called <u>Thinking Outside The Box</u> to make people aware of the 10/40 Window and the unreached people groups. I also edit a magazine called *The Unpublished WORD Journal* because I want to make people aware of the need. I have found out that many people are not going or not praying or giving, not because of disobedience or rebellion but because of a lack of information. So I am working to give out that information.

I resigned a church at fifty-nine years of age, after thirty-five years as that church's pastor, to get involved in unreached people groups that do not have the Word of God. We need to play catch-up. We are never going to reach the unreached if we keep putting the emphasis where we have been putting it. We need to give more, and go farther, and pray better.

God loves the unreached, as well as the reached. Please keep in mind that emphasizing the unreached is not a matter of value

HE IS WORTHY

nor of fairness but of obedience. The unreached are not more valuable than the reached in the eyes of God but they do deserve the same privilege of knowing Him. He also wants worship from them forever in Heaven. They are in His image, loved by Him, included in the cross, and the blood of Jesus can cleanse their sins also. The real calamity of unreached people is not only that they will die and go to Hell, but that God will not be honored and glorified and worshipped by that part of His creation.

When we say that people are unreached, we mean that <u>they have not been reached with the God-approved remedy for their sins</u>. There is only one God-approved remedy for our sins, and that is the cross. The gospel is not the best way to be saved; it is the only way to be saved. The gospel is exclusive. That is why the world hates us. We believe that the gospel is the only way, and that Christ's name is the only name.

How do we know that the cross is God-approved? We see in Isaiah 53:11, *"... He shall see the travail of His soul, and shall be satisfied."* So God is satisfied with the work of Christ on the cross. How do we know that? I know it because of the resurrection. When Christ was resurrected, it was God's way of saying, "I'm releasing you (Jesus) from your assignment, (salvation of men) because you have completed it." I also know it because in October of 1958, I experienced it.

We have the only remedy, but sometimes when we talk about unreached people, we get the wrong idea.

I. <u>They are not unreached as far as a knowledge of God is concerned</u>. They know that there is a God out there somewhere that is angry with them because of their choice of life style, and they have to do something to buy off His wrath.

Look at Romans 1:20. *"For the invisible things of him from the creation of the world are clearly seen, being understood by the things that are made, even his eternal power and Godhead; so that they are without excuse."* There is enough information in creation to convince anyone, except for a few "educated"

Americans, that there is a God. They are without excuse if they try to deny it, because they have creation all around them just like you do.

You drive down the road and see the trees die in the fall and come back in the spring; that is a picture of the resurrection. You see how good God is, how beautifully He makes things, and that is a testimony of God. Unreached people live in the midst of creation in the same way we do, so they know there is a God.

They also know there is a God because of their conscience. In verse 15 of Romans 2, we read about *"their conscience also bearing witness, and their thoughts."* The unreached are not ignorant as far as knowledge of God and His existence, but they have little knowledge of God with regard to His moral character.

Missionaries who go to unreached people are not going there to tell them there is a God or that God is offended by their lifestyle. They know there is a God and we are not even going to tell people that God is offended by their lifestyle. Anthropologists have said that they have never found a group of people on earth, no matter how deep in the jungle, that did not have a sacrificing system. That would tell you two things about those people: that they believe in a "God" who deserves worship, and they believe that their conduct of choice has offended that God. That is why they offer the sacrifice, because they believe there is a God who has been offended.

By the way, both of those points are true. There is a God, and He has been offended. I know that, and they know that. So they are not unreached with that knowledge. Missionaries go to tell them that God loves them and how to satisfy that God, through our faith in the death, burial and resurrection of Jesus Christ.

II. They are not unreached with the effects of the fall. What are those effects? Total depravity. Go back to Genesis 6:5-7. This is the story of the Flood, which we all know very well. It is also after the fall.

A. *"And God saw that the wickedness of man was great in the earth, and that every imagination of the thoughts of his heart was only evil continually. And it repented the Lord that he had made man on the earth, and it grieved him at his heart. And the Lord said, I will destroy man whom I have created from the face of the earth; both man, and beast, and the creeping thing, and the fowls of the air; for it repenteth me that I have made them."*

So after the fall, man got so bad that God said, "I'm sick of man. I'm sorry I made man. I'm going to destroy man and save only Noah." That was the effect of the fall back then.

B. In Romans 1, we see that the unreached people have also been affected by the fall. I think Romans 1 describes those Gentiles that have not the law. In verse 20-21, they are referred to as *"without excuse: Because that, when they knew God, they glorified him not as God ..."*

Verse 24: *"Wherefore God also gave them up ..."*
Verse 26: *"... God gave them up ..."*
Verse 28: *"... God gave them over ..."*

If you read Romans 1:20-32, you will find twenty-one terrible accusations against man just as there were against the people in Noah's day. The difference is that God said He would not destroy man again. Because of the fall, man became very vile. In one verse it says that they became idolaters.

Look at verse 23. *"And changed the glory of the uncorruptible God into an image made like to corruptible man, and to birds, and fourfooted beasts, and creeping things."* Go to the mission field and you will find out how true that verse is. I have seen people defend rats, monkeys and cows as gods. They worship all kinds of grotesque gods.

Later in this chapter, we read how they became full of lust: men with men, women with women, idolaters, adulterers, lesbians and homosexuals. That describes the effects of the fall, but the sad thing is in verse 20, it says, *"... they are without excuse."* They made their own bed. Some might say, "Well, if they made their own bed, let them lie in it. If that is what they have chosen, then leave them alone."

C. Before you decide that, you might want to look at Romans 3:9. This verse is not talking about the Gentiles without the law, but Jews and Christians who have the Word of God. *"What then? are we better than they?"*

You take one of those idol worshippers on the other side of the world, scrape off all of that paint and filth from his body, and you will find your relation in there. You will find one of your distant cousins. You will see that they are made of the same mud from which you are made. We are no better than they are until we meet Jesus.

I see pictures, and I think, "Dear God in Heaven, how can anyone get to that state? How can they worship pornographic stone images? How can they throw their children to the crocodiles in the river? How, when a man dies, can his tribe burn his widow? How do you get to that point?"

The answer is back in Romans 3:9-19. *"What then? are we better than they? No, in no wise: for we have proved both Jews and Gentiles, that they are all under sin; As it is written, There is none righteous, no, not one: There is none that understandeth, there is none that seeketh after God. They are all gone out of the way, they are together become unprofitable; there is none that doeth good, no, not one. Their throat is an open sepulchre; with their tongues they have used deceit; the poison of asps is under their lips: Whose mouth is full of cursing and bitterness: Their feet are swift to shed blood: Destruction and misery are in their ways: And the way of peace have they not known: There is no fear of God before their eyes. Now we know that what things soever the law saith, it saith to them who are under the law: that every mouth may be stopped, and all the world may become guilty before God."*

We are as guilty as they are before God. We may have nicer clothes, be better educated, smell better, and act better, but we

HE IS WORTHY 53

are as guilty before God as they are. So you might say, "Preacher, let 'em alone! If they chose that, let them live that." But I say to you, we do not want that for ourselves.

Paul continues in verses 20-22 and then summarizes it all in verse 23. *"For all have sinned, and come short of the glory of God."* The Gentile without the law has sinned. The Jew with the law has sinned. We are all guilty before God.

Let me ask you: Do you want to be left alone? The only difference between us and them is that God, in His grace, put the gospel in our midst. They are who they are because they do not have the gospel, and so they are the products of their own imaginations and their own deities.

God, in His grace, put you in the way of the gospel. He gave you a Book. He put you in a church. You are children of God, and God takes pleasure in you, but only because you have what they do not have. Without the gospel, you would be as pagan as they are, and so would I. You may not like that. I do not like it very much myself, but it is a fact.

In Acts 16, the apostle Paul is on a missionary trip. Look at verse 6. *"Now when they had gone throughout Phrygia and the region of Galatia, and were forbidden of the Holy Ghost to preach the word in Asia ..."*

Where are the unreached? Where is the 10/40 Window? It is located in Asia, the Pacific Rim, China, India, and northern Africa. You should put a big black mark on that verse, because it shows that Paul wanted to go where the unreached people are now and the spirit of God forbad him from going there.

Verse 7 says, *"After they were come to Mysia, they assayed to go into Bithynia: but the Spirit suffered them not."* Those places were in the direction of Asia. The Spirit said, "Don't go in that direction."

Now look at the next three verses: *"And they passing by Mysia came down to Troas. And a vision appeared to Paul in the night; There stood a man of Macedonia, and prayed him, saying,*

Come over into Macedonia, and help us. And after he had seen the vision, immediately we endeavoured to go into Macedonia, assuredly gathering that the Lord had called us for to preach the gospel unto them."

Paul wanted to go to Asia, but the Holy Spirit said, "No, go the other way." What was in the other direction? Europe.

These verses decided who today's unreached people would be. If God's Spirit had let Paul go to Asia, Bythinia and Mysia, do you know where we would be today in the West? We would be without the Bible, without a church, and without the gospel. We would be without God.

Who decided that Paul should bring the gospel in the direction of Europe? The same One who decided that most of us reading this book would be of European descent. The gospel came to England, Germany and France. The Pilgrims brought it to Holland, then to North America. Who decided to bring the gospel this way? God did.

Who decided that I would be born to parents in West Virginia? It was not me; I was not up there casting a vote. If I had, I would not have made it West Virginia (for those of you from that great state, that is a joke).

Who decided from which way the gospel would come? Who decided that you would be put in the way of the gospel? Most of you were born in the United States or Canada, where there is more of the gospel than anywhere on earth. That is because centuries ago, the Holy Spirit told Paul, "Go that way."

It is by the grace of God that you are not among the unreached. We would be an incredibly hard people today if we did not try to get the gospel to those people after God decided to let us have it first.

Jesus said, "Go into the all the world and preach the gospel." Now He just wants you to give what has been given to you. We do not have the gospel because we are better. We are made of the same mud as they are; we are just as guilty before God as they are. When God made the choice, it was not between the bad and the good, or the better and the best, but it was simply a choice of His grace.

In October of 1958, Dallas Billington preached to a couple of young people who had just gotten married. I had been a bus kid. My wife and I were able to be saved because we were in the reached part of our world.

Now would you decide out of graciousness, thankfulness, and appreciation to God to help Him now reach some people whom He did not get before but that He still wants to save? They are not overlooked in the Great Commission. Every time you read about the Great Commission, it refers to the world, to the nations, to all creatures, and to the uttermost.

Let us not overlook them. They are included. God may have come to you first, but He does not want to stop with you. Why are they not overlooked? Because they are in God's image. They are loved by God, they can be cleansed by the blood of Christ, and God wants to be worshipped by them.

When I first was saved, I surrendered to be a missionary to Lebanon. For forty years, God never let me do anything about it, but He never let me forget it either. Now I am finally able to fulfill that commitment.

Look at Revelation 5:9. This is one of the verses that changed my life. *"And they sung a new song, saying, Thou art worthy to take the book, and to open the seals thereof: for thou wast slain, and hast redeemed us to God by the blood out of every kindred, and tongue, and people, and nation."*

God's desire is to be worshipped by someone from every kindred, tribe, tongue and nation. You need to stand up today and say, "I am privileged to help God realize His desire."

Go to Revelation 7:9. *"After this I beheld, and, lo, a great multitude, which no man could number, of all nations, and kindreds, and people, and tongues, stood before the throne, and before the Lamb, clothed with white robes, and palms in their hands."* This passage talks about God being worshipped by people from every nation. We should want to help Him fulfill His desire.

For years, fundamentalists had no awareness of the unreached, no strategy to reach them and no vehicle through which to work. As a young preacher, I heard other preachers be unkind to groups like New Tribes Missions and Wycliff Bible Translators. Those folks go in and live 20 or 30 years with a tribe to give them a Bible. I have heard fundamentalists speak ill of that. I am not a supporter of these groups. We have never been involved with them because we disagree in more than a few areas.

But now, *FirstBible* International gives you another vehicle to use if you will get on board. It gives you a strategy if you will apply it. It gives you awareness to create a burden. Would you, out of gratitude to God, help us reach the unreached?

THE EXPECTATION

"And I say also unto thee, That thou art Peter, and upon this rock I will build my church; and the gates of hell shall not prevail against it."

Matthew 16:18

"But ye shall receive power, after that the Holy Ghost is come upon you: and ye shall be witnesses unto me both in Jerusalem, and in all Judea, and in Samaria, and unto the uttermost part of the earth."

Acts 1:8

My mother and father are both in Heaven now. When I was a youngster, my mother always told me every time I walked out the door of our home, "Be careful." That was her last command to me as I departed. When I was 50 years old, she still said that to me. Sometimes what people say when they are leaving really has significant meaning.

When Jesus said to go into all the world and preach the gospel, He said to go into Jerusalem, Judea, Samaria and the uttermost. We need to be clear concerning **what He expects** from us, and we need to understand clearly that it **can** be done.

What kind of God would we have if He told us to do something we could not do, and then held us accountable because we did not get it done? That would not be a very just God, would it?

Let me suggest to you that Jesus made very clear what He wanted accomplished. Five times in forty days, from His resurrection until His ascension, in a glorified body — five times He made it clear. Five times in some form He said, "Go into all the world and preach the gospel." I used to think He said it once, and everybody heard it and wrote it down. That is not how it happened at all.

He said it in Matthew 28:18-19, right out of the grave. *"All power is given unto me in heaven and in earth. Go ye ... and, lo, I am with you."*

He said it again in Mark 16:15 — *"... to every creature."*

He said it again in Luke 24:47 — *"... among all nations."*

He said it again in John 20:21 — *"... as my father hath sent me, even so send I you."*

He said in Acts 1:8, *"But ye shall receive power, after that the Holy Ghost is come upon you: and ye shall be witnesses unto me both in Jerusalem, and in all Judaea, and in Samaria, and unto the uttermost part of the earth."*

He states it very clearly for a total of five times in forty days in His glorified state. The command is pretty clear.

Not only did He make clear what He wanted done, but also

HE IS WORTHY

that He would provide what was necessary to get it done. In Matthew 28:18-20, He promised us the **power** we need, and He also promised His **presence**. We cannot go anywhere carrying the gospel outside the bounds of His power and His presence.

He has promised **provision**. He said in Philippians 4:19, *"My God shall supply all your need according to His riches in glory by Christ Jesus."* If we go, we have needs, and He supplies those needs through others. He has also provided enough **personnel** to do the job. It is clear what He wants done, and it is just as clear He assumes the burden of supplying whatever it takes to do it. We may be misdirecting the things He is supplying for the Great Commission, but never the less, it is there although we may not be using it for the assigned task.

So God expects whole-world evangelism. In spite of His having made it clear what He wants done, there are still 3.2 billion unreached people. I do not mean people who have rejected Him; I mean people who have never been reached so that they can reject Him.

In missions we frequently use the term "near-neighbor evangelism." Most of you got saved out of near neighbor evangelism. Someone close to you, in your culture, reached you. It may have been a Sunday school teacher, or a preacher, or your neighbor, or a work mate, or your parents. Someone in your culture reached you with the Gospel because they already had the gospel.

There are more than three billion people on earth who cannot be reached by near neighbor evangelism. It is not that they have rejected the gospel; they have never had it. Jesus made it clear that we are to go into all the world and preach the gospel. Yet 3.2 billion people have never seen a Bible. They have never been in a church, never heard a Christian song or a sermon, or never heard the name of Jesus.

There are more than 6,000 languages without an entire Bible. To our knowledge, out of about 6,500 languages and dialects on this planet, there are only 273 with the entire Bible. Can you believe that? The good news is, because of the prayers and support of many of you, in early 2005 we presented the 274th group with its own copy of the Word of God.

At one time, when I read the word "nation" in the Bible, I thought it was referring to a geopolitical entity with geographical boundaries, a government or a standing army. About 250 or so of those exist in the world. That is not what the Bible meant at all. The word "nation" in the Bible means a group of people who have a natural affinity for each other, the same language and basic ethnic background, the same culture — a group of people among whom the gospel or any other truth can move unhindered. When the gospel is hindered from moving because the people are not alike, that is another "nation" in the Biblical sense.

There are approximately 24,000 people groups in the world. About 6,000 of those have yet to receive the gospel. That is staggering. There are also 12,000 independent, fundamental Baptist churches in the United States alone. Wouldn't it be wonderful if every church in America just adopted a people group? When you figure in all churches of every denomination (including those in which you would not want to have membership), there are 600 churches for every unreached people group.

So the Lord made it clear that we are to reach the nations, give the Bible, and go into all the world. Let us make certain we understand the command.

We have done a good job in some places in our Jerusalem. We are doing pretty good in our Judea and Samaria also. I do not think Samaria represents anything geographically as much as it represents a subculture within the culture (like prisons or rest homes in this country).

<u>We are not doing well when it comes to the uttermost; we want to and we must do better.</u>

Do you know how much money the average church gives

for the half of the world that does not have the Bible? Only two-tenths of 1% of every mission dollar is for the unreached. For every dollar collected for missions in churches in the United States, two-tenths of one cent goes to the unreached half of the world, and 99.8 cents goes to the reached half. We need to reassess that.

We have 3,000 missionary families from the United States that are out in the world preaching the gospel. Thirty percent of our missionaries are in five countries. Ten percent of our missionaries are in Brazil. That does not mean there are too many in Brazil; that is only one for every 500,000 people in that country. We are doing a good job; we are just not doing enough. We need to reassess where we are.

<u>Lest I sound negative, I would have you know that the Baptists are sending the most missionaries of any major denomination; 21 percent of all career missionaries on foreign soil are Baptist, and 22 percent of the Baptists are into cross-cultural church planting. That is the best of any denomination. It takes 7.1 denominational Baptist churches to produce one missionary but it only takes 4.1 fundamental Baptist churches to produce one missionary. That is not good, but it is better than the denominational Baptist.</u>

For many years, America per capita was the greatest missionary-sending nation on earth. Now we are 16th. What does that mean? It means that someone is not clear as to what God wants done or those who are clear are not obeying.

Here is the other part of the problem. Not only are we not doing it as we should, but there is also not even a plan for getting it done in a great number of churches. The average church has no plan or strategy to reduce the unreached. That does not make sense. I thought He was clear about this.

I am trying to get you to the point where you are consumed by the fact that half the world does not have the gospel and it is up to us to get it to them, because He said for us to go do it.

I was in 52 churches in 2004. That is probably too much

for someone my age. In going to 52 churches, here is what I found: It is the Lord who builds the church. He uses people, but He is the one who will get the job done. I also found very few people who are burdened by the fact that so much of the world is unreached.

Are you burdened? Are you praying for nations whose names you cannot pronounce? I really believe we have come to this place in our history for such a time as this (to reach the unreached).

Fifteen years ago, I did not know a Muslim from a Minnesotan. I did not know anything about the 10/40 Window. Now there are so many of us thinking in that direction, for so many reasons, and that is where the unreached people are.

Do you know how the gospel gets into a country? You will never believe this. I always thought the best way to reach China, or Spain, or Togo, was to win someone from that country and let that person go back and reach them. The problem is that, as a rule, they do not go back. Once they get a taste of our way of life, they want to stay here. Instead, the gospel is usually carried into a country by soldiers. In Japan, the Philippines, and Korea, some Americans who went there the first time as soldiers in the early part of the 20th century went back later as preachers.

Now we are fighting another war. You can have whatever opinion you like about the situation in Iraq, but the fact remains that we are fighting a war in the 10/40 Window. When that war is over, many of those soldiers who were there in combat will go back carrying the cross. I want to have Bibles ready when that army marches out. The other way the gospel gets in is through commerce. Once again, you can have your own opinion about that, but the fact remains that we are developing trade relations in the 10/40 Window which will allow a door through which the gospel will be able to enter.

We need to have a strategy. We need to be very clear about what the Lord wants.

HE IS WORTHY

The Great Commission did not start with Jesus. I always thought it did. He had every right to start it, but He did not. The Great Commission started before the world began.

In Titus 1:2, Paul wrote, *"In hope of eternal life, which God, that cannot lie, promised before the world began."* God discussed eternal life before the world began. That is where it started.

The Great Commission was also in the Old Testament. The first conversation God had with fallen man in the Bible, in Genesis, was where He promised Adam and Eve that their seed would bruise Satan's head. *"And I will put enmity between thee and the woman, and between thy seed and her seed; it shall bruise thy head, and thou shalt bruise his heel."* (Genesis 3:15) God was promising a way back for those who came short of His glory, which is all of us. He made that promise to man back in the Garden of Eden, on the evening of the first day of man's fall.

In the opening verses of Genesis 12, He founded a nation. Do you know why He created Israel? In the previous chapter at the Tower of Babel, God was unhappy with man's attempt to be great it his own eyes, so He scattered them — 70 different nations, 70 different people groups. Then He called out Abram in Genesis 12 and said, *"And I will make of thee a great nation ... and in thee shall all families of the earth be blessed."* What He was saying here was, "I have scattered the nations. Now I will make a nation that will gather them back together with the Gospel."

Israel was not designed so that God could <u>exclude</u> the rest of the world, but so that He could <u>include</u> them, because He loves us.

Look at the story of Jonah. It was about a man who did not want to take part in God's plan to reach Nineveh. It was a wicked city that the Jews hated (sounds like the 10/40 Window). God wanted to reach them, and Jonah said, "I'm not going to be a part of that." The issue is not whether Jonah did it, but that God wanted it done, because God has always had a global heart.

In another place in the Old Testament, God asked, *"Whom shall I send? and who will go for us?"* Isaiah answered, *"Here am I; send me."* I am telling you, God had a global heart long before the Great Commission was laid out in the New Testament.

God made it clear in Genesis 3:15, Genesis 12, Isaiah 6, books of Jonah, Ruth, Esther and many other places in the Old Testament; He wanted the world invited back to recovery. He has made it abundantly clear the church is to be the organization/organism through which He would be doing it. Look at Matthew 16:18. *"And I say also unto thee, That thou art Peter, and upon this rock I will build my church; and the gates of hell shall not prevail against it."* Read the second part of that verse again. What Jesus is saying is that nothing can stop the church if God has assigned a task and the members of the church take it up.

Has the Lord assigned the church a task? Five times in forty days, Jesus said to go into all the world and preach the Gospel. Can we do it? If we will take it up, we can. If the gates of hell cannot prevail against us, we can get it done.

I was raised in West Virginia and in Colorado, and I know what a gate is. You know what it is, too. A gate is put up in a certain place to stop progress. The Lord said, "If you will take up the task I have assigned you, nothing will stop you. I am promising my **power**, my **presence**, and my **provision**, and if you provide the **personnel**, nothing will stop you."

What happened? Why, after 2,000 years, is half the world still unreached? Maybe we have not taken up the task.

It has previously been done. Look at Romans 1:8. *"First, I thank my God through Jesus Christ for you all, that your faith is spoken of throughout the* **whole** *world."* Some theologians think that means their faith was spoken of throughout their "then-known world." For discussion's sake, I will assume that is true. Have we spread our faith throughout our known world in 2005?

I have been on the mission field in places where they never had the gospel but they had Singer sewing machines. I have seen places where the people had Bayer aspirin but never had the Bible. I have seen Coca-Cola and Pepsi signs in places where no one had the Water of Life. May I suggest to you that, whatever this verse in Romans means, it shows that they did it better than we are doing now.

Now go to Romans 16:19. *"For your obedience is come abroad unto all men."* Have we gotten our gospel "abroad to all the men" of which we know? Of course not. There are 3.2 billion who have not yet received it.

A little farther down, verse 26 says, *"But now is made manifest, and by the Scriptures of the prophets, according to the commandment of the everlasting God, made known to all nations for the obedience of faith."*

All nations, all of the people groups they knew about at that time, received the gospel. I have in my home a book a couple of inches thick that lists 12,000 people groups without the Gospel. There are 12,000 people groups of which we know.

Read Colossians 1:5-6. *"For the hope which is laid up for you in heaven, whereof ye heard before in the word of the truth of the gospel; Which is come unto you, as it is in all the world ..."* The rest of the world got as much as they got. That is not true with us today, is it?

Look at verse 23 of the same chapter. *"If ye continue in the faith grounded and settled, and be not moved away from the hope of the Gospel, which ye have heard, and which was preached to every creature which is under heaven ... "*

Folks, we have problems. We are not doing as well as they did, and they did not have all that we have. We need to shake ourselves and realize that He wants the whole world reached, and we cannot be stopped if we decide to do it. Let us be clear what He wants done, and let us be clear on the fact that it can be done.

To do it, we have to change our motivation. We have got to stop doing it for **them**; they are not worth it. I heard someone on television say, "The cross proves our worth." No, the cross proves that we are good for nothing. It also proves God's love. Since we can never love them that much, we will not reach them unless we start doing it for the love of Jesus.

Jesus asked Simon Peter a question three times in John 21.

Verse 15: "*... lovest thou me more than these? Feed my lambs.*"

Verse 16: "*... lovest thou me? ... Feed my sheep.*"

Verse 17: "*... lovest thou me? Feed my sheep.*"

It is love for Him that helps us reach out to them. Paul said in 2 Corinthians 5:14, *"For the love of Christ constraineth us."* Why did Paul go through so much in his life? Because he loved Jesus. Now if we love God, and He puts us in a certain area, we will start loving those people. It starts with a love for God. When you give, you need to do it for God's sake, not for their sake.

We have to become creative. If we keep doing what we have been doing, we are going to have what we already had. To reach that other half of the world, we are going to have to do some new things.

One of our problems is that we think we are doing it the way Paul did it. We are not doing it Paul's way. When was the last time you rode a boat to another country or walked across a continent? We are carrying the message Paul carried, but not by the method he used.

Some of you think it has always been done the way it is being done now, but it has not. William Carey did not do it that way, and neither did Hudson Taylor. We have to decide that it is time to make a paradigm shift.

We have to play catch-up. We must move into an emergency mode. We cannot include the uttermost as just another missions line item and ever hope to catch-up. I am challenging churches to give ten percent of their mission dollar to the Scripture needs of the unreached. You say, "Why so much?" Well, it still leaves 90 percent for everything else, but mainly because we are playing catch-up. We have to get more people, more money and more Bibles out there faster than we have in the past. We are far behind in that half of the world.

We must develop methods to create awareness. My first book, <u>Thinking Outside the Box</u>, was written to create awareness. I edit a magazine called *The Unpublished WORD Journal* for that same reason.

A lot of churches are not involved in the needs of unreached people because they never thought about it. No one ever challenged me to be burdened about the unreached. In my 35 years as a pastor, I had missionaries come in all the time, and they always challenged me about where they were going. I did not blame them for that. Then the people who surrendered after hearing those missionaries would go to those same places. No one ever said, "Hey, there's half a world without the gospel."

One day, it dawned on me that there was half a world without it. That is why God orchestrated my resigning from Bearing Precious Seed. The emphasis, at least while I was there, was to print Bibles, New Testaments and Scripture portions to go where people already have Bibles. These are called trade languages. That is not wrong, but someone needs to go where the Bible is not available.

Missionaries cannot do it without lay people who have a world view. We need to move missions from the "called" to the "commanded" column; I am going to stop using the word "called" when talking about missions. You might be called regarding <u>where</u> to go, but not as far as <u>what</u> you are to do. You might be in the United States with a world view to help me reach India; you do not have an option as to what your goal is to be — world evangelism. So let us stop talking about having a call and just say that we are all commanded.

You need to find out where you fit in the command. A dear lady told me the other day, "I don't have much money, but I can pray." Is that important? You better believe it is.

Some can give, some can pray, and some can go; but we are all commanded to help reach the world with the gospel.

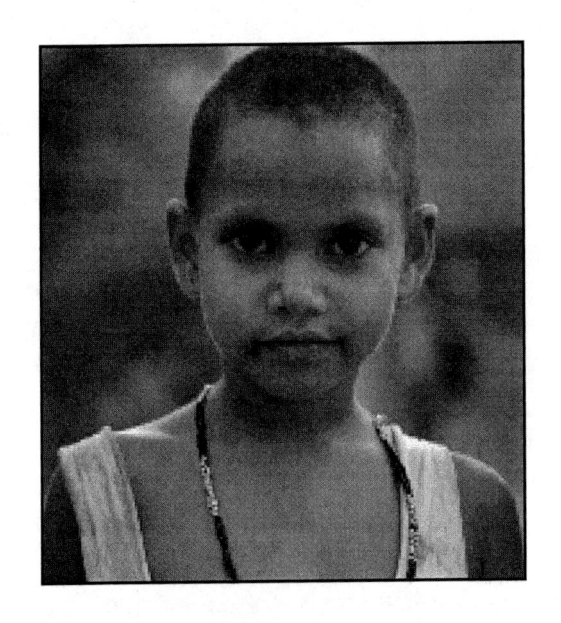

YOUR PURPOSE

"And he had two wives; the name of the one was Hannah, and the name of the other was Peninnah: and Peninnah had children, but Hannah had no children."

I Samuel 1:2

I have a real burden for those who do not have the Bible. My wife and I have given our lives, having quit our ministry of thirty-five years as pastor of a wonderful church, to try to get the Bible to those who do not have it.

Romans 15:4 says, *"For whatsoever things were written aforetime were written for our learning, that we through patience and comfort of the Scriptures might have hope."* What that verse says is that the things written aforetime (that is the Old Testament) are written for our learning.

I also have a burden for those who have the Bible. I am convinced that the average Christian in the average church operates in a few choice places; a few choice books, and a few choice chapters. We have sixty-six books, and God wants us to study them all.

Now go back to I Samuel 1. This is an example of something written aforetime for our learning. You are probably asking, "What would this passage in I Samuel 1 have to do with missions?" There are actually two things.

One is faith. Hannah is the first woman in the Bible to have a recorded prayer. It is a long prayer. In fact, there are two prayers recorded in the first two chapters of I Samuel.

The other is purpose. Look in verse 2, where it says, *"Hannah had no children."* That is very important. In verse 6, it says that this made her fret. In verse 7, she wept. In verse 8, she was grieved. In verse 10, she was *"in bitterness of soul ... and wept sore."* In verse 15, she even spoke of her *"sorrowful spirit."*

Why did she have that kind of emotional content to her character? Because she had no children. This is not a mother fretting over being barren. This is a woman grieving over not being able to fulfill her purpose in life. A woman in Israel would never go to war. She would never be in the parliament. She would never have a chance to sit on the throne. A woman in Israel knew that her contribution, her purpose, was to provide a king or a soldier or a statesman and give her nation what she could not do

HE IS WORTHY

herself. Her way of contributing to Israel's present and future good was through giving her nation a man child. And a woman who was barren was missing her purpose in life. Hannah was grieved because she was not completing what she was put here to accomplish.

In verse 20, it says that she had a son. She was finally able to fulfill her purpose. I am interested in what she did between verse 2 and verse 20 to reverse her condition.

Some of you reading this do not have what you need to fulfill your purpose for God in this world. If there is something we can perform to realize our God-given purpose, we need to do it. So it is a good idea to study Hannah and see what she did.

Keep this in mind: Hannah was already a good woman. By the same token, many of you are good people. You love God. You are interested enough to be reading this book. Hannah and Elkanah were good people, but they still were not fulfilling God's purpose.

Look at verse 3. It says that they *"went up ... yearly to worship and to sacrifice."* They were regular in attendance, regular in worship. They gave their offerings.

Verse 4 shows that Elkanah was a good husband. *"And when the time was that Elkanah offered, he gave to Peninnah his wife, and to all her sons and her daughters, portions."* He gave portions to his wives and children. Verse 5 says that he loved Hannah. *"But unto Hannah he gave a worthy portion; for he loved Hannah ..."* Verse 7 tells us that they went to the Lord's house every year. *"And as he did so year by year, when she went up to the house of the LORD ..."* They were good people.

We are good people just like they were, but are we fulfilling our God-assigned purpose? What is that purpose? It is to provide for the church both a good present and future.

As far as missions is concerned, most of us are not going, and most of us should not go. I used to preach and try to make everyone who did not go feel guilty. The truth is that God is not leading a lot of you to go. But we still have the same purpose whether we stay or go, and that purpose is world evangelism through a world-view. So we need to find out where we fit in. Do we go to the far corners of the world, or do we stay and pray and give so others can go?

I. Now go to verse 11, where Hannah *"vowed a vow."* We will call that "faith promise." Her vow consisted of three things.

First, she was willing to give what she had to get what she did not have. She did not have a boy, but she did have a body. I do not mean to be unkind here, but she was not asking to adopt or to be a foster parent. She said, "I want to bear a child."

Second, she promised a specific amount. She said that if God gave her *"a man child,"* she would give him back to God. It was specific. You need to decide what you are going to do specifically toward your purpose. Are you going to go? Are you going to pray? Are you going to give? What specific thing are you going to do for world evangelism?

No one has a right to be exempted from participation. "But I'm a kid." Sorry, if you are saved, you are part of the program. "But I'm an old man like you, Brother Keen." You're still not exempt. Moses was eighty and I was fifty-nine when God called us to missions. Age does not exempt you; you might not go, but there is a part for you.

So Hannah gave what she had, to get what she did not have. She asked for a specific amount — one male child. She assigned a specific purpose to it — to give him to the Lord. For us, the purpose is missions. There is a specific amount for each of us, and we are all to have a part in it.

Now go to verse 18. *"And she said, Let thine handmaid find grace in thy sight. So the woman went her way, and did eat, and her countenance was no more sad."*

Verse 6: *"... her adversary also provoked her sore, for to make her fret."*

Verse 7: *"She wept, and did not eat."*

HE IS WORTHY

Verse 8: *"... why weepest thou? and why eatest thou not? and why is thy heart grieved?"*
Verse 10: *"... in bitterness of soul ... and wept sore."*
Verse 15: *"... I am a woman of a sorrowful spirit."*
Verse 16: *"Out of the abundance of my complaint and grief have I spoken."*

At this point she was still barren. Look at the previous verse: *"Then Eli answered and said, Go in peace: and the God of Israel grant thee thy petition that thou hast asked of him."* She had been asking for a man child. Eli told her she could have one, and she started rejoicing while she was still barren. Why? Because now she was going by the Book instead of her body, by what she heard from God instead of what she saw.

We need to get to the place where we believe God is going to do something wonderful in our church, in our families, and in our lives, and just start rejoicing over that. God is ready to do something great. If He does not do something great for you, it is not because He does not want to do it. Hannah started rejoicing because she knew God would do what He said He would do.

Look at verse 19: *"And they rose up in the morning early, and worshipped before the Lord, and returned, and came to their house to Ramah: and Elkanah knew Hannah his wife; and the Lord remembered her."* Now we see Hannah reversing her condition from barren (verse 2) to birthing (verse 20).

Whatever you promise beyond what you have, God has to get it to you by some means. He is not going to come down and knock on your bedroom window every Saturday night and hand it to you so you can offer it on Sunday. Instead, God is going to take something you have been doing and make it more productive than it has ever been. He has to get it to you somehow.

Elkanah and Hannah had been in their relationship for quite a while, but it had not been fruitful where children are concerned. Now, in verse 19, that same relationship has become more fruitful than it had been because *"the Lord remembered her."* What did

God remember? He remembered her promise.

Read verse 11. *"... if thou wilt indeed look on the affliction of thine handmaid, and remember me, and not forget thine handmaid, but wilt give unto thine handmaid a man child, then I will give him unto the LORD all the days of his life ..."* She had asked for a male child and promised to give him to God, so that is what He gave her.

Look at verse 20. *"Wherefore it came to pass, when the time was come about after Hannah had conceived, that she bare a son, and called his name Samuel, saying, Because I have asked him of the LORD."* What she got is what she promised. Verse 27 says, *"For this child I prayed; and the LORD hath given me my petition which I asked of him."*

I am not talking about dominion theology, like these television preachers who say, "Send me a dollar and I'll give you ten." I am not talking about "name it and claim it" or "blab it and grab it." What I am saying here is that God will bless obedience. Hannah wanted something she did not have, and she promised to give it back to God once she got it. *" ... And the Lord remembered her."*

What does God remember? He remembers what you promised Him. In the last part of verse 20, Hannah names her son Samuel *"because I have asked him of the Lord."* Hannah received for what she asked. In verse 27, she says, *"For this child I prayed; and the Lord hath given me my petition which I asked of him."* Faith Promise is, quite simply, God responding to your commitment.

I have a sermon entitled, "God Works Out Of A Suggestion Box." When I was in Bible college, I worked at Fisher Body in Pontiac, Michigan. They had a suggestion box on the wall, and if you thought of anything while you were working that was a good proposal for the company, you put it in the box. If the company acted upon your submission, you received a bonus.

Have you ever thought of how many times in the Bible God

HE IS WORTHY

did something because someone suggested it? It was Peter who suggested walking on the water. It was not the Lord's idea. Peter said, "I have a suggestion."

Why don't you tell God what you would like to do? Why don't you let Him honor your prayer and force you outside your comfort zone? Promise Him something big enough that when it gets done, He gets the glory. Our problem most of the time is that we live and work in a safety zone, and when there is a problem, we work it out. Who gets the glory then? We do. But if you would ask for something that God has to do, then He will get the glory.

But the great thing about Hannah's Faith Promise is not the son she received, but the revelation she received from God for having participated. Beginning with the first verse of chapter 2, she is praying with praise and rejoicing. She did that for the first 10 verses. She had started living a life where God was allowed to be God, and she was seeing Him in a way she had not formerly seen Him.

Many of us have gotten bored because we have not seen God move in a great way in our lives. We sing the songs in a ho-hum way, and we listen to the sermon just to get a little whiff. We do not expect God to do anything great. We are not impressed by God anymore. I would rather fail trying to be impressed by God than just stay safe on the shore, without experiencing any different opinion of God than what I had when I got saved.

Hannah was able to praise God like she did because she had allowed Him to do something in her life that previously had not been done. Would you allow God to put you in a place to do something He has not up to this time done for you before?

II. Look at I Samuel 2:18-19. *"But Samuel ministered before the Lord, being a child, girded with a linen ephod. Moreover his mother made him a little coat, and brought it to him from year to year, when she came up with her husband to offer the yearly sacrifice."*

As she brought him that coat every year, there was always something different about it. It was bigger each year, because he was growing. He grew because Eli, the man of God, fed him well. If you are in a place where the man of God is feeding you well, then you should do more this year than you did last year. If you are in a good church, you gather three or four times a week, put your feet under the table and let the man of God spread the feast. So you are growing in your faith. If you are reading your Bible and participating in family devotions as you should, then you are growing even more. For Jesus' sake, you need to allow yourself to make a bigger Faith Promise this year, because you are bigger in your faith this year than last year.

That is what happened with Samuel. Verse 21 of chapter 2 says, *"And the child Samuel grew before the Lord."* In verse 26, *"And the child Samuel grew on."* In verse 19 of chapter 3, *"And Samuel grew."* Make your Faith Promise offering based on two factors: your growth factor, and your faith in God.

III. Go back to I Samuel 2:20. *"And Eli blessed Elkanah and his wife, and said, The Lord give thee seed of this woman for the loan which is lent to the Lord."* Because Hannah got involved in Faith Promise, made a commitment, and followed through with it, then God blessed her. She had five more children, three sons and two daughters. God will bless you when you make that kind of commitment.

Can you imagine what the neighbors said about Elkanah and Hannah when they gave up Samuel? "That preacher is just asking too much from that young couple. They do not have much and he wants them to tithe and give to the building fund." Those are the kinds of people who criticize your pastor and people like me who ask you to give to special projects.

But that is not the end of the story. Hannah is in the supermarket and meets a neighbor. She cannot hold it in any longer. "Guess what? Elkanah and I are expecting again. It's a boy."

All the neighbors are excited. They probably throw a shower

for her. Then it is not too long before Hannah is in another store, meets another neighbor and announces another pregnancy. More congratulations (but not another shower), then another little one comes a year or two later. Suddenly Hannah has three little children at home. By the time the fifth one shows up, as cited in verse 21, the neighbors are saying, "Could you put up a fence, buy a sand box and a teeter-totter and keep those blessings at home?"

I was thrown out of Milford, Ohio, because of the blessings of God. Our church had buses, bad parking, traffic jams, and the neighbors signed a petition. God was blessing because we were giving to missions, and He blessed so much that the neighbors finally asked us to leave the neighborhood. So we went six miles out in the country, bought twenty-five acres, and had our own party.

Look at Philippians 4:19. We all know this verse; we can quote it and have claimed it. But do we know the context of it? *"But my God shall supply all your need according to his riches in glory by Christ Jesus."*

For the context, go back to verse 16. *"For even in Thessalonica ye sent once and again unto my necessity."* This is the apostle Paul, a missionary, writing to a supporting church. He is telling them about how they have helped with his needs, so God will in turn supply theirs.

There are a lot of churches out there with big needs. Some of them need to build and make more room to grow. The worst thing a church could do is cut back on missions to erect its buildings. Giving to missions is what will build a building.

In my thirty-five years as a pastor, we constructed $10.5 million worth of buildings — all debt-free. While we were doing that, our mission offerings kept growing to the point where we were giving $500,000 a year to missions and had forty-three families on the mission field. We were a beehive of missions activity, and God just kept expanding our boundaries. While we were taking care of others' necessities, God took care of our own needs.

This promise in Philippians is not just for the needs of the church, but it applies to families' needs as well. Luke 6:38 says, *"Give and it shall be given unto you; good measure, pressed down, and shaken together, and running over, shall men give into your bosom."*

That is what Hannah had. She was running over with children in the house and in the yard. God is not going to give you just what you have given; if He did, we might as well keep it. The farmer plants a seed to get back the thing he planted and much more. Whether it be your house, your church, or yourself, God is committed to bless you in that manner. If we believe the whole Bible, then we know that God is the God of supply and resupply. If you do not think so, ask that little boy with the loaves and fishes.

My prayer to God is that we would get right so we can do right. Doing right means doing more.

YOUR PART IN HIS PROGRAM

"And it came to pass, that, as the people pressed upon him to hear the word of God, he stood by the lake of Gennesaret, And saw two ships standing by the lake: but the fishermen were gone out of them, and were washing their nets. And he entered into one of the ships, which was Simon's, and prayed him that he would thrust out a little from the land. And he sat down, and taught the people out of the ship. Now when he had left speaking, he said unto Simon, Launch out into the deep, and let down your nets for a draught. And Simon answering said unto him, Master, we have toiled all the night, and have taken nothing: nevertheless at thy word I will let down the net. And when they had this done, they inclosed a great multitude of fishes: and their net brake. And they beckoned unto their partners, which were in the other ship, that they should come and help them. And they came, and filled both the ships, so that they began to sink. When Simon Peter saw it, he fell down at Jesus' knees, saying, Depart from me; for I am a sinful man, O Lord. For he was astonished, and all that were with him, at the draught of the fishes which they had taken: And so was also James, and John, the sons of Zebedee, which were partners with Simon. And Jesus said unto Simon, Fear not; from henceforth thou shalt catch men. And when they had brought their ships to land, they forsook all, and followed him."

Luke 5:1-11

An old man traveling a lone a highway
Came in the evening cold and gray
To a chasm deep and wide.
The old man crossed in the twilight dim,
For that stream held no fear for him,
But when he reached the other side
He built a bridge to span the tide.
"Old man," said a fellow pilgrim near,
"You're wasting your strength building here,
For your journey will end with ending of day
And you never again will pass this way."
The builder lifted his old gray head.
"Good friend, on the road I have come," he said,
"There follows after me today
A fair-haired lad who will pass this way,
And this stream, which has been naught to me,
May to that fair-haired lad a pitfall be."

You may have heard that poem entitled "The Bridge Builder." That is what it is all about. Those who have gotten across are to help those who have not yet crossed.

Is that not what soul-winning and world missions is all about? In much the same way, we are to give the gospel as the bridge to bring people to God. In 2,000 years, it has only reached half the world with the news that there is a bridge to God, the cross. We still have a long way to go.

The goal of your church, and every church, should be "everyone doing something." No one who is a member of the Lord's church is exempt. It does not matter if you are retired, on a walker, an entrepreneur or uneducated, a young adult with a spouse, a single parent with children, a teenager, or a young child with an allowance. No one is "4F." You are to be a part of His program; you are to do something. No Christian is relieved from the responsibility and privilege of world evangelism. You

HE IS WORTHY

will be glad and happy at the Judgment Seat of Christ that you were allowed to have a part.

After we grasp the concept of "everyone doing something," we can and should move to "<u>everyone doing something more than the year before.</u>" Each of us should do more than the year before, for four reasons:

1. There is <u>more to do</u>. There have never been more lost people on planet Earth than there are today.

2. There is <u>more that can be done</u>. In this age of modern technology with such things as: satellite, radio, TV, e-mail, Web sites and computers, not to mention our printing abilities, and communication. Add to that our transportation capabilities, and the fact that we live in the most open world in the last 100 years, there are ways to get the Word of God to the far corners of the globe in which no one had ever dreamed.

3. There is <u>more to you</u>. For many of you, there is more to your church numerically than there was. There is also more to you spiritually as a Christian. If you have been sitting under the right kind of Bible preaching each week for the past year, there is no way you could not have grown bigger in your faith.

4. There is <u>less time to get it done</u>. We are dying, the lost are dying, and Jesus is coming.

In the story we read in Luke 5, they went from nothing to abundance. They started out washing their nets on empty decks of empty ships, but they ended up with so much that they needed to call for help.

It is obvious from this story that Jesus had a **program**, to get the Word of God to the people. Look at verse 1. *"And it came to pass, that, as the people pressed upon him to hear the word of God, he stood by the lake of Gennesaret."* If He was to see His program of getting the Word of God to the people accomplished, Peter, James and John must have a **part** and He made it clear in verse 2: *"And saw two ships standing by the lake: but the fishermen were gone out of them, and were washing their nets."*

This would not be done without others having their part.

He also has a program for us today. It is called world evangelism, and we are called to have a part. All of the other good ministries and good things we get involved in our local church serve only to prepare us to do His program, but they are not the program.

Five times in forty days, from Jesus' resurrection until His ascension, He established the program for His church (Matthew 28:19-20, Mark 16:15, Luke 24:47, and John 20:21). Each of those times, He said in some form to go into all the world and preach the gospel. So it seems pretty clear that His program for us is world evangelism. That is the purpose for the church, and we are to have a part.

The gospel has never been where a man did not put it; there are still multitudes who need it. God knows where they are. He loves them, they are included in the cross, under the blood and made in His image, but they are lost and without hope. Half of the world does not have the gospel, a Bible or a church, but they are not being reached because so many of us are not having a part in His program. We learn from this account in Luke that in order for us to have a meaningful part in His program we must consider several things:

I. **SHORE** — represents where we are standing at present in relationship to His program.

Look at where these men were in verses 1-2, and where Jesus found them. *"And it came to pass, that, as the people pressed upon him to hear the word of God, he stood by the lake of Gennesaret. And saw two ships standing by the lake: but the fishermen were gone out of them, and were washing their nets."* They were *"standing by the lake"* (what we call the **shore**).

You need to consider where you are standing at present in relationship to His program of world evangelism. Where are you: in your finances, in your prayer life, in your goings? At this point the important thing is not "Is where I am standing right or

HE IS WORTHY

wrong?" I just want you to identify <u>where</u> you are standing in your giving, praying, or going. As a preacher I need to ask myself what do my sermons say about my stance in relationship to His program. As a pastor what does the ministry emphasis of my church say about my standing in relationship to His program.

II. <u>SHORE, **SHIPS** — represent what we have to contribute into His program.</u>

If the <u>shore</u> represents where we are standing, the <u>ships</u> will represent what we have to contribute to His program of world evangelism. There are several references to a ship or ships in this passage.

Verse 2: *"And saw two ships standing by the lake ..."*

Verse 3: *"And he entered into one of the ships, which was Simon's ... And he sat down, and taught the people out of the ship."*

Verse 7: *"And they beckoned unto their partners, which were in the other ship, that they should come and help them. And they came, and filled both the ships, so that they began to sink."*

So I would suggest that ships are vitally important to the program. These men had what Jesus needed, and these things would have to be given up if they were to be a part of His program.

Verse 11 says, *"And when they had brought their ships to land, they forsook all, and followed him."* So if the shore represents where you stand, the ships signify what you have to contribute.

You have three things you can contribute.

A. The first is your **silver**. Everyone in the Lord's church should do something monetarily for the cause of Christ. Before you were saved, someone was doing something monetarily that would contribute to your salvation. While you were still lost, someone was paying the bills at the church, putting gas in the buses, paying for radio or television broadcasts, and a host of other things. So it seems that common decency would lead you to do likewise so that someone else can be reached. They may not even care about God (much as you may not have cared before you were saved), but we need to take the light to them anyway so they might be saved.

B. The second thing you can contribute is your **seed**. I am talking about your children. I have been preaching for more than 40 years, and I have seen hundreds of parents bring their children to the altar soon after they were born and dedicate them to God. Too many parents today are raising their children with an eye toward creature comforts, for education, positions and titles, corner lots with large houses, and cars and boats.

How many of us have really given our children to God for world evangelism or for ministry? I know we cannot put our children in the ministry, but we can make them aware from a young age to pray about what God would have them do. They should be available. From where do missionaries come? We do not get them from a farm or a laboratory somewhere. They come from us, our churches and our homes.

C. The third thing we can give is our **selves**. Let me ask you a question. Do you know of a chapter and verse in the Bible that says the Great Commission, the greatest thing a church can do, should be left up to a bunch of novice kids right out of college? I thank God that those kids are willing to go, but why should we leave it up to them alone? Maybe the effect of the gospel has not rippled fast enough around the world because it was not meant to be left just in their hands.

I was nearly sixty years old when God called me to be a missionary. I had been a pastor for thirty-five years. You can read many times in the Bible about how those who already had a "call," "got the call." Take Jonah, for instance. When he got the call to go to Nineveh — which he did not heed at first — he was already called to be a prophet. Isaiah was a prophet when he got the call. Peter was a successful entrepreneur when he got the call. Some of you reading this book may need to stop exempting yourself just because you are in mid-life, or because you are already in some level of ministry. Your age is not an excuse.

III. <u>SHORE, SHIP, **SHIFTING** of position is required.</u>

Now look at verses 3-4. *"And he entered into one of the ships, which was Simon's, and prayed him that he would thrust out a little from the land. And he sat down, and taught the people out of the ship. Now when he had left speaking, he said unto Simon, Launch out into the deep, and let down your nets for a draught."* You might want to call this part of the story **shifting positions** or **shoving off**. The Lord was telling them, "If you're going to be what you ought to be, then you can't stay where you are any longer."

That is what this book is partly about — getting you to move, or shift your position, as in verse 3 (*"... thrust out a little from the land ..."*) or verse 4 (*"... Launch out into the deep ..."*). I do not know how much, or how far, you should move. (You being where you are at this point does not mean you have been out of His will up to this point.) That is between you and God. My job is to get you to the point where you are willing. Let God give you your new instructions and assignment.

He first told the men in the ships to launch out a little. Some of you probably do not have to go very far from where you are right now or where you have been. You cannot stay in the same place for long and be where He wants you to be. Maybe you are giving a certain dollar amount, or have become involved in a church ministry like singing in the choir, or teaching a Sunday school class. You may just be led to give a few dollars more or go to new ministry location in your own church and your community (*"thrust out a little"*). You might be called upon to do a lot, *"launch out into the deep"* and go to Greenland, Cuba, Haiti, Bible college or somewhere else to reach that part of the world with the gospel.

Wherever He wants you to be, whether it is near or far, little or much, remember that He is in the boat with you. So why not just decide that you are going to reposition yourself according to His will? Even if you do not know how far you will go, pick up the anchor. Start cultivating an attitude of obedience and willingness. Do not be afraid of it.

Please note that when these events in Luke 5 took place, Peter had been with Jesus for seven months. You probably already know that Jesus only had a 3 1/2-year ministry on earth. So it was not like Peter was just starting to get on board. He was already growing in his faith, trying to be like Christ and live right. Jesus said, "I want you to go a little farther." No matter where you are today, you probably are not as far along as you need to be. It is time to launch out.

IV. <u>SHORE, SHIP, SHIFTING, **SURRENDER** — where Jesus is trying to bring you to in His program</u>.

Look at verse 5. They had *"toiled all the night, and have taken nothing."* Jesus said, *"Let down your nets for a draught."* What did Peter say? "Nevertheless at thy word I will let down the net." This is **surrender**. You could also call it overcoming conventional wisdom or living above humanistic thinking. They had been using traditional methods and been unsuccessful, and when Jesus came along and told them what to do, Peter told Him what had happened the night before as if Jesus did not know already. "Lord, that's not how you do it," he said, but then he added, *"Nevertheless."* He did it because it was what his Lord told him to do. He knew that he was the pupil and Jesus was the teacher. So he let down the net. That is surrender.

We have to overcome conventional wisdom. You will never do what God wants you to do if you think that way. You must get the mind of Christ. You cannot approach a supernatural job in a humanistic mindset. You will have to accept that what God is asking of you does not exactly add up in your head. But remember that He is the Creator, and He makes decisions based upon what He knows He is going to do, not what you know.

When He pushes you out of your comfort zone to the place you are not in control your first instinct will be to say, "Lord, this isn't going to work." God wants to do something in your life that is not being done.

I graduated from high school in 1957 in a suburb of Akron, Ohio. My wife and I were in the same class, having gone to school together since seventh grade. Out of 52 in my graduating class, academically I ranked 52nd. When I got my diploma, the faculty snickered.

I did not like school at all. I wrote inside my textbooks, "In case of fire, throw away." I got into more trouble with my dad through the years over my report card than anything else. So when I got out of high school, I was never going to school again. I did not even want to drive by that place.

My wife and I got saved the second Sunday of October in 1958 (one year after graduation). We started going to church for every service, tithing, reading our Bible, and teaching Sunday school. God started to move in my heart about going back to school and then into full-time ministry. I said, "God, let me remind you about something you forgot. I toiled for twelve years in school just to find out I do not have much upstairs."

When I talked about it with my wife, I said, "You would not want to go with me anyway." She said, "I believe in you. I'll go." I could not talk her into not going, so I decided to go.

I told my adult Sunday school teacher about my plans for Bible college, and he said, "Take a leave of absence from your job. Don't quit your job completely." That was not too encouraging. He was telling me that he did not think I would make it. I told him, "I'm quitting my job and burning all of my bridges. If there were a way back, I wouldn't come back. I'm going full speed ahead with no retreat possibilities."

As a testimony to the goodness of God, I graduated in 1964 at the top of my class at Midwestern Baptist College. He knew His plan even though I did not. He knew what was in their future. All you need to do is surrender, and then one day you can tell your grandchildren or your pastor, "Look at what God has done."

V. SHORE, SHIP, SHIFTING OF POSITION, SURRENDER, SHARED PARTNERSHIP.

Look at verse 7 and consider the **shared partnership.** *"And they beckoned unto their partners, which were in the other ship, that they should come and help them. And they came ..."* Do you know why they need help? It was because they were doing the will of God. I have always known if you do <u>not do</u> the will of God, you are going to get into trouble. I knew that the first day I was saved. What I did not know for a long time was that <u>doing</u> His will would also get you into trouble. Look at what it did to Peter. He got more fish than he could fry, and his boat started to sink. He was in trouble, and he started calling for help, all because he did the will of God.

Your pastor has more going on than he can do because he is doing the will of God. So he asks people like you to help him by taking a Sunday school class or become an usher or doing something else. When you agree to do that you are partnering with him. This kind of partnership is necessary because people are doing things beyond their abilities.

The men in Peter's boat shouted, "Help!" Another boat heard their cry and came to help. Today we have missionaries who are crying for help as well. They have surrendered to do something they cannot do without your help, your partnership, if you please. They come to your church partly to get into your wallet, but do not dare think less of them for that. If you do, why don't you go? God bless them for going.

Now we see a strange truth in this passage. While Peter was shouting for help, where was Jesus? He was in the boat. Peter could have turned and said, "Lord, would you mind picking up a corner of the net? Could you help with the anchor? How about making the fish jump into the net a little slower?"

Jesus is with us in the boat today, too. He could walk into your church auditorium Sunday and preach the most glorious message you have ever heard. He could make a stack of gold bars appear and hand them to a missionary to meet a financial need. But He wants us to do these things for Him. There is no question that God has it to give; He just wants to give it through us. We should thank Him for wanting us to have a part, so we can fare well at the Judgment Seat.

Imagine standing before God one day and hearing Him say, "I want you to meet someone. This person was saved because you sent someone to reach him." You see a child of God standing there in ethnic garb and the skin color of his birth. God is glad he is there and you are, too.

VI. SHORE, SHIPS, SHIFTING, SURRENDER, SHARED PARTNERSHIP, **SHOCK** OF PARTICIPATION.

In verse 9, we see **shock**. *"For he was astonished, and all that were with him, at the draught of the fishes which they had taken."* They were shocked at how much was left in that which they had given up on as hopeless.

During my years as a pastor, we never had a church split, but a lot of churches sprang up in our area that I felt like I had started. Whenever someone would leave our church to go somewhere else, what they were really saying was, "Your church no longer has anything for me." What they did not know was that, while they went to another church, someone was usually coming from that church to ours.

You might be surprised at what is left in your church if you would do church God's way. You might be calculating what you and the rest of your church are already giving to missions, or a building fund, and wonder if there is anything else to give. You would be shocked at what God could do in your church if you would do missions God's way.

We built buildings debt-free with a market value of $10.5 million at First Baptist Church of Milford, Ohio, while I was the pastor. It was during those times that our Faith Promise giving grew the fastest. A church of 1,000 gave $500,000 to missions each year while in a building campaign. At that same time, we had more young people surrender to the ministry and to the mission field than at any other time. God just came in and blessed everywhere. So do not shut the door and think that it can not happen where you are. God could do something shocking things at your church or in your life if we will let him be God.

Peter and his coworkers did not have to go to another sea, lake, or find another boat. They worked with what they had under obedience to Jesus, and they were shocked at what God did. Only God knows what your church can do for world evangelism if you decide to let God lead in what you do.

VII. SHORE, SHIPS, SHIFTING, SURRENDER, SHARED PARTNERSHIP, SHOCK, and finally **SUCCESS** in the program.

I caught a lot of fish as a pastor, some of which I should have thrown back. I caught some piranha that just about ate me alive, and some big-mouthed bass (if you know what I mean). Most of us tend to equate success with the fish we catch, the surrender we see, the ships we get invested, or the people we get involved; but the real success here is in verse 8. *"When Simon Peter saw it, he fell down at Jesus' knees, saying, Depart from me; for I am a sinful man, O Lord."*

Your success from here on is not based on how much you give, but on what you see. Peter saw a lot of miracles during his first seven months with Jesus. When he fell on his face and became obedient, he saw Jesus in a way in which he had never seen Him. Real success is to let Him work in your life and show Himself to you in a way in which you have never seen.

If you are saved, you want to know the Lord better. The more you know Him, the more you find you do not know. It is a cycle I cannot really explain, but I enjoy it.

Our problem is that most of us are just bored. I do not find many people delighting in the Lord. If you do not believe me, just go listen to people in your church talk to each other in the lobby before and after the service. We fight a lot because we are bored and fighting at least breaks that boredom. A lot of people become charismatics, even though it is wrong, because it is fun. We are living out of duty instead of a life of delight (which I guess is better than nothing), but we are just bored.

The best thing to get you out of your boredom is to see Him in a new way. How wonderful it would be to leave church Sunday not talking about the great song you heard or the great sermon, but saying, "What a great God I saw today." Most people think that if the preacher gives a better sermon or the singer sings a better song, we will see a better God. All of that is just icing on the cake. What led Peter to a new revelation of Jesus was *new obedience* to Jesus. If you allow Him to do something new in your life, you will get a better vision of Him than you have ever had.

Nearly all of the miracles Jesus performed utilized human assistance, not because He could not do them alone, but because other people were helped by their participation. He raised Lazarus from the dead, but He asked someone else to roll the stone away. He turned water into wine, but He asked someone else to bring some empty jugs. He fed 5,000, but He asked someone else to pass out the bread and fish. He wanted others to do something so that they would think more of Him.

The lost need Him. He could do it without us, but then you would not have the joy of seeing Him exalted in a new way in your life. Obey Him, and let Him become more real to you today. **SUCCESS.**

GETTING ON THE SAME PAGE

"When Jesus then lifted up his eyes, and saw a great company come unto him, he saith unto Philip, Whence shall we buy bread, that these may eat? And this he said to prove him: for he himself knew what he would do. Philip answered him, Two hundred pennyworth of bread is not sufficient for them, that every one of them may take a little. One of his disciples, Andrew, Simon Peter's brother, saith unto him, There is a lad here, which hath five barley loaves, and two small fishes: but what are they among so many? And Jesus said, Make the men sit down. Now there was much grass in the place. So the men sat down, in number about five thousand. And Jesus took the loaves; and when he had given thanks, he distributed to the disciples, and the disciples to them that were set down; and likewise of the fishes as much as they would. When they were filled, he said unto his disciples, Gather up the fragments that remain, that nothing be lost. Therefore they gathered them together, and filled twelve baskets with the fragments of the five barley loaves, which remained over and above unto them that had eaten. Then those men, when they had seen the miracle that Jesus did, said, This is of a truth that prophet that should come into the world."

John 6:5-14

Jesus performed thirty-two miracles during his earthly ministry, starting with the transformation of water into wine and ending with the raising of Lazarus from the dead. The miracle depicted in this passage was the biggest of the thirty-two, as it helped the most people at one time.

It was so important that it was the only miracle mentioned in all four gospels (Matthew 14, Mark 6, Luke 9 and here in John). It was one of only two miracles that Jesus referred to at a later point in His own ministry. It was one of the few miracles that required the participation of all twelve disciples to accomplish it.

Despite the scope of this supernatural achievement by Jesus, we find in this story one person who was reluctant to have a part. His name was Philip. It is a bit surprising that Philip was so reluctant, because:

1. Jesus made it very clear what He wanted to do. There was no doubt as to His will in this situation; He wanted to feed every person there.

2. This was a legitimate need. The people gathered here were hungry.

3. It was also clear that Philip was to have a special part in this miracle because of his special position as one of the 12 apostles.

In summary, Philip was not on the same page to help with Jesus regarding this massive assignment that Jesus obviously wanted to see accomplished.

Before I am too hard on Philip, let me suggest that this same scenario is carried out thousands of times every week across America. The church is full of men and women just like Philip. Consider this:

1. The Lord has made it clear what He wants done, having clarified the Great Commission for us five times within forty days before His ascension. We are not to feed five thousand; we are to reach six billion. It is obviously a big job.

2. It is a legitimate need. Let me ask you a question, "Is the gospel the best way to be saved?" No. It is the only way. Some people think you can be saved because of ignorance. "If they don't know, then they're all right." Jesus said in John 14:6, *"I am the way, the truth and the life: no man cometh unto the Father, but by me."* Every man who has not heard the name of Jesus Christ is lost.

So while it is a big job and a legitimate need, He has made it clear that it can be done.

3. We are in a position to get it done. You can drive down the street almost anywhere in America and see hospitals and cemeteries for dogs and cats, while thousands of cities around the world lack such facilities for human beings. We have so much in this country and we are in a position to do something so meaningful. Why are we so reluctant? Why do we hold back and refuse to step out? Why are we not, like Philip, on the same page with Jesus when it comes to the Great Commission?

You might say, "Brother Keen, who is to say we are not taking part?" It is easy to see that we are not on the same page with Jesus by the way we spend our money.

1. The average fundamental, independent Baptist church gives two-tenths of one cent out of every mission dollar to unreached people groups. The other 99.8% goes to the half of the world that has already heard the gospel. It is time the other half heard it as well.

You have probably heard the phrase, "There's an elephant in the room." I used to laugh when I heard that even though I had no idea what it meant. I found out later that it means there is something big going on but no one wants to talk about it. If I were speaking in your church and an elephant walked into the auditorium, I would be remiss not to point it out. Someone could be killed or seriously injured, and it would be my responsibility to make you aware of the situation. Well, there is something big going on in our world in that 3.2 billion people are without the gospel. I want to make you aware that we need to be doing something about it.

2. The assignment of our personnel also shows that we are not on the same page with Jesus. There are far fewer people going to those areas that are still without the gospel.

3. The relatively low attendance at the average missions conference shows a general lack of interest in the area in which our Lord has the most interest.

Everywhere I travel I go into the bookstore and say, "Please show me your section on missions." I can tell you almost without exception what the girl behind the counter will say in response, "I'll have to ask the manager." Then the manager will say, "We don't have a section on that, but we have a book or two on missions down here under the shelf on soul winning or discipleship." That is great, but it is not missions. Why are they not selling what is most important to Him? Because they are selling for what you, the customer, is asking. Could I say we are not on the same page?

You do not hear any sermons on world evangelism outside of a missions conference. When was the last time you read a sermon about missions in a periodical? It takes four independent fundamental churches to produce one missionary. I do not think we are all on the same page; some not even in the same book.

I thought He was the Father and we were His children. When I was a kid, my dad made the rules and enforced them. If it was important to him, it did not matter if it was important to me. I just had to get in line.

Do you know how many missionary families there are around the world coming from fundamental churches in America, carrying the story of God's own dear Son? Fewer than 3,000. There are 12,000 fundamental, independent Baptist churches. To some of you, three thousand families might sound like a lot. It is nothing. It takes four churches to produce one missionary; that is embarrassing.

HE IS WORTHY

4. Very few people are involved in Bible translation. There are about 6,000 languages and dialects on this planet, and fewer than 400 of them have the whole Bible. If you reduce the world to a global village of 100 people, only <u>4</u> of them would have a Bible. Only <u>12</u> would have the entire New Testament, and <u>30</u> would have some portion of Scripture. That would leave the other 54 with <u>nothing</u>.

So you cannot really be too hard on Philip. His attitude is replayed hundreds of times each week in our churches across America. God is trying to get people to go further, give more and pray better, and they are holding back, for whatever reason. It is just not that important to them.

As I read this story, I asked myself, "Why did Philip hold back?" Here are some reasons he may have had:

I. <u>Philip was not on the same page because when his commitment was requested, he did not factor God into the equation</u>. Look at verse 5. Jesus is asking for a commitment. *"Whence shall* **we** *buy bread that these may eat?"* With that statement, Jesus was offering the chance for partnership in this project.

Then we see Philip's response in verse 7. He turned atheistic, which many of us often do. He said the bread was not sufficient. If he was talking about just himself and the bread, then he spoke the truth. He forgot to factor in the God of creation.

Jesus said, "What can **we** do?" Philip said, "What can **I** do?" You can do nothing without Him. With Him you can do anything He calls upon you to do.

He wants to partner with you and your church in world evangelism. He is not asking you to do it by yourself. He is saying, "Whence shall **we** 'go into all the world'?" Look at Matthew 28:19-20. *"Teaching them to observe all things whatsoever I have commanded you: and, lo, I am with you alway, even unto the end of the world. Amen."*

After all, it was the Lord's idea. He came up with the plan. It was not the disciples' idea to feed the multitude, nor was it any of the hungry people who suggested it. It was the Lord Jesus Christ who said, "This is a project that I want to be involved in with you." It was His idea.

II. <u>Why should Philip believe that Jesus would partner with him on this project? For one thing, Philip had His Word on it from the moment Jesus said, "We."</u> Do we have His Word on it today? After He said to go into all the world, He followed it up with, *"Lo, I am with you alway."* We have His Word that if we will go, so will He. We will have His presence, His power, and His provision.

Now consider whose idea it was to go into all the world with the gospel. The apostles did not get together and say, "Lord, we had a meeting while you were in the tomb, and we decided that if you ever got out, we should do this." No, Jesus burst out of the tomb and said, *"All power is given unto me ... go ye."* It was His idea, and He has offered partnership.

III. <u>Philip also forgot to apply what he knew about the Bible.</u> Philip was a Jewish man raised in a Jewish nation by Jewish parents. It would be impossible for him not to know the Old Testament, not to mention that he had walked with Jesus for months. He no doubt knew of Moses feeding all of those people in the wilderness. It would have been a good idea for Philip to think before he answered Jesus about feeding the five thousand and consider whether something like this had ever happened previously. He might have remembered how Moses led a million (some say three million) Israelites out of Egypt. In just a few days they got hungry and grumpy, but Moses got alone with God and those folks ended up with all the food they needed.

Do you have any idea how many meals that is? One million people (there were actually more) eating two meals a day for forty years. If every man ate six ounces of food, that was sixty-seven tons of food a day. Over forty years, it comes out to more than two billion meals that God provided through Moses. Philip

HE IS WORTHY

should have thought, "We're just feeding 5,000 one time for one meal. We're getting off easy here."

If God did that for Moses, for Philip, and for others in so many places in the Bible, why not let Him do something like that for you? You can trust Him because, like He said, *"I am the Lord and I change not ... the same yesterday, today and forever."* He did it then, and He will do it now. I will let Him lead me now because of what He did then. Why don't you?

IV. <u>Another thing Philip could have done was just consider his own life</u>. Of the thirty-two miracles Jesus performed, this was the tenth. He had already turned water into wine, healed an impotent man, stilled a tempestuous sea, healed a centurion's servant, raised Jarius' daughter from the dead, healed a blind man and a dumb man, and cast a legion of devils out of a man. Philip had been present for most, if not all, of that. He should have thought, "Wow, the Lord didn't just work in Moses' life and in the Old Testament. He is working here in my life also. Why would He stop now?" He did not stop. After He fed this crowd, He had 22 miracles to go.

Many of you who are reading this are in churches that could not have gotten where they are today without seeing and being involved in some miracles. I have some good news for you. God was not finished when he fed the 5,000. Philip lived to see him do twenty-two more, and He still has miracles for us regardless of how many or how large His miracles in the past were.

Let us get on the same page. We are talking about people being saved from Hell, God being glorified, the cross of Christ being effective, and the Word of God being published.

In reading this passage, we should learn from Philip:

A. <u>That good men can be wrong</u>. He was saved, belonged to a good church, had a good pastor, knew the right doctrine, was separated, faithfully attended the programs — but when it came to this big project, he was not on the same page with Jesus.

The fact that you are reading this suggests to me that you are probably a lot like Philip in the fact you are a good person by the church's standards. Let me say to you as kindly as I know how, if you are not for world evangelism, you are as wrong as he was.

B. <u>Good people who do wrong can get right (and usually do)</u>.

Look at how Philip got right. Verse 11 says, *"And Jesus took the loaves; and when he had given thanks, he distributed to the disciples ... except Philip."* Does your Bible say that? Mine does not. That verse indicates to me that all twelve disciples were involved in the project. That means that at some point Philip said, "I shouldn't have been thinking that way, Lord. I want to have a part in this, too." He realized that his reluctance was misplaced.

Go to verse 13. *"Therefore they gathered them together, and filled twelve baskets with the fragments of the five barley loaves, which remained over and above unto them that had eaten."*

It does not say eleven baskets were filled; it says twelve. How many disciples were there? There were twelve. Philip was one of them. He told Jesus, "Lord, let me distribute some bread and fish, and give me a basket to gather up what is left." He got back on the same page because good men who do wrong can usually get right.

C. <u>Maybe the reason this good man got right was he simply decided to follow the leadership of his pastor, Jesus</u>. "Lord, I don't understand all of this, but you are my pastor and I'll follow you." The greatest thing a pastor can have is "leadable" people. Your pastor may want you to stretch out in ways in which you have never thought. You might not understand it, but get behind him anyway and follow his leadership.

D. <u>It is possible Philip got back on the same page because he saw so many other good men doing it</u>. When Jesus started this project, eleven of the twelve disciples were in favor of it. Now think about your own situation. If you are wondering about whether to do something for God and a lot of good people are doing that, you could be wrong. Philip was looking for a way out, while Andrew was looking for a way in. Philip may have gotten right because he did not want Andrew to make him look bad. Or maybe he felt if a lad could be such a large part of this project, certainly an Apostle should be. We do not know why he got right, but we do know that he did.

E. <u>The last thing I want you to notice here is that Philip finally saw the large picture</u>. The real issue is not food, fishes or faces. That is all he saw at first — humans being helped by humans. By verse 14, he saw the real thing. *"Then those men, when they had seen the miracle that Jesus did, said, This is of a truth that prophet that should come into the world."*

The "those men" of verse 14 refers to the 5,000 men in verse 10. The real victory in this story is not that fishes and food fed faces. It is the fact that as a result of this miracle, Jesus occupied a new level of exaltation in people's hearts. It happened when those men said in verse 14, *"This is of a truth that prophet ..."* Now obviously He is more that a prophet but up to this miracle, to them, He was just a man. What we see is an escalating opinion of Him.

Your obedience in world evangelism can have the same effect. Not only will people get saved; they will also see God and Christ in a new way. If you do not love them enough to feed them, do you love Him enough to see Him exalted like that around the world? Jesus is seen in a new way by those who are reached for Him. That is the big picture.

A man once said to me, "<u>I am not afraid to fail. What I fear is that I will succeed in something that does not matter to God</u>." There are many things in which you can be successful that do not matter to God. What does matter to Him is that the gospel reaches the world. After all, it is about His Son.

GOD WANTS YOU TO BE GOOD AT GIVING

"*Moreover, brethren, we do you to wit of the grace of God bestowed on the churches of Macedonia; How that in a great trial of affliction the abundance of their joy and their deep poverty abounded unto the riches of their liberality. For to their power, I bear record, yea, and beyond their power they were willing of themselves; Praying us with much intreaty that we would receive the gift, and take upon us the fellowship of the ministering to the saints. And this they did, not as we hoped, but first gave their own selves to the Lord, and unto us by the will of God. Insomuch that we desired Titus, that as he had begun, so he would also finish in you the same grace also. Therefore, as ye abound in every thing, in faith, and utterance, and knowledge, and in all diligence, and in your love to us, see that ye abound in this grace also. I speak not by commandment, but by occasion of the forwardness of others, and to prove the sincerity of your love.*"

2 Corinthians 8:1-8

In verse 7, the last phrase is, *"See that ye abound in this grace also."* If you read this in context, you see that the apostle Paul is talking about them abounding in the grace of giving. The next three chapters deal with abounding in the grace of giving.

Write this down, or do whatever you have to do so that you never forget it: God wants you to be good at giving. We act like God requires it of us and then trips us up while we try it. He wants us to be good at giving.

Every time I speak at a missions conference, I try to show how God wants every one of us to have a part in world evangelism. Some people, perhaps in your church, will go. That is their part. The others will be staying. The ones who are supposed to go need to go. The ones who stay need to pray and pay. We all have a part.

I sign my letters, "Minister of Munitions." Everyone asks me why I do that, and it shows the general lack of information about history. Winston Churchill, one of my non-biblical heroes, had as much to do with the Allies winning World War II as any man on earth. During that war, he signed his letters, "Winston Churchill, Minister of Munitions." When he was asked why, he said, "I feel that my greatest job in this war is keeping ammo on the front lines." Similarly, I have tried since 1959 to keep ammo in the form of the Word of God going to missionaries on the front lines.

Let me say this as kindly as I can. You must not put down this book, or leave the doors of your church after a Sunday service, without going, praying, or paying. If you leave church without participating, you do so without the umbrella of God's blessing. God wants you to be good at giving. One reason I believe that is because of how thoroughly He deals with the subject of giving in the Bible. Your relationship with your earthly possessions is the most commonly used sermon topic of the greatest Preacher who ever walked on this planet, the Lord Jesus. He preached more on that than any other subject.

He talked about the positive side of it in Luke 6:38. *"Give, and it shall be given unto you; good measure, pressed down, and shaken together, and running over, shall men give into your bosom. For with the same measure that ye mete withal it shall be measured to you again."* What He is saying here is that when you give, you get. I do not think He meant that selfishly; He was simply saying that if you are part of the program, you will be part of the blessing also.

Both sides of giving are covered in 2 Corinthians 9:6. *"But this I say, He which soweth sparingly shall reap also sparingly; and he which soweth bountifully shall reap also bountifully."*

There are many other examples. Jesus talked about the lad who gave and got, and the widow who gave of her oil and received. There is no doubt that if we take part in giving, we become part of the cycle of blessing. Why does He talk about this so much? He is trying to draw you into a giving pattern.

There is also a negative connotation. Look at Adam. He did not give, but he took. Did he profit? No.

Achan took. Did he profit? No.

Ananias and Sapphira took. Did they profit? No.

I was a pastor for thirty-five years and we had a wonderful ministry. One day I told the head usher, "Go down to the sign shop and get some Ananias and Sapphira bumper stickers printed. Then watch who doesn't give and put the bumper stickers on their cars: 'We are Ananias and Sapphira. Get out of our way. We are about to die.'"

I did not really do that, but I wanted to sometimes. My point is that God clearly shows the positive aspects of giving and the negative aspects of not giving. He also says that He is the Lord and He never changes. In other words, "As I acted then, I will act now." I have the same God that Abraham had.

I. You cannot wait for everything to be just right before you start doing right.

Look at the beginning of our text. *"Moreover, brethren, we do you to wit of the grace of God bestowed on the churches of Macedonia; How that in a great trial of affliction the abundance of their joy and their deep poverty abounded unto the riches of their liberality."* Verse 2 shows that things were not going so well. In the midst of so many problems, they did what they were supposed to do; they gave.

I have discovered that things will never get exactly right for us to give without some kind of pain. You can never wait for things to get that good. You want to wait for one child to get out of braces, or for another to finish college, or whatever financial burden you think you have.

"Brother Keen, I can't do it now because I am in a bit of a bind right now."

"Brother Keen, you want our church to give so much money for missions and we're in a building program."

You exempt yourself so many times, you never get to the place where you are not exempt.

I spent most of my life worrying about getting my kids out of braces or through school, and now I am trying to think about my retirement. You never get to the point that you have a free ride. You might as well decide, "I need to do it now, because Jesus wants to save them <u>now</u>. They're dying and going to Hell <u>now</u>, so I'll just do right, right now. This is regardless of the need at my house." The church at Macedonia decided to do right even though everything was not just right.

II. The basic ingredient in giving is our willingness, not our wealth.

That is where so many of the television preachers go wrong. They are trying to get you wealthy. "Send a dollar and God will give you ten." I'm going to write the next guy who says that and tell him, "You send me a dollar and let God give you the ten." I doubt he will go along with that.

There is a popular philosophy called "name it and claim it." You could call it "blab it and grab it." All of these people are trying to work on your greed for wealth. Paul wanted to work on your desire to be willing.

Look at verse 3. *"For to their power, I bear record, yea, and beyond their power <u>they were willing</u> of themselves."* He was saying that they did right because they wanted to do right. They were not doing right because they were wealthy, but because they were willing.

Now look at verse 11. *"Now therefore perform the doing of it; that as there was a <u>readiness to will</u>, so there may be a performance also out of that which ye have."* They were performing properly because they had a willingness to perform properly.

Verse 12: *"For if there be first a <u>willing mind</u>, it is accepted according to that a man hath, and not according to that he hath not."*

Verse 19: *"... and declaration of your <u>ready mind</u>."*

May I suggest to you that we need to work on our willingness rather than our wealth. So I ask myself, "How can I be willing?" There are two ways to do this.

First, look at examples of other churches who are giving. That is what Paul did.

In the first two verses of chapter 8 to the Corinthians, he talked about the example of the Macedonians.

Then, in the first three verses of chapter 9, he wrote to the Macedonians about the giving of the Corinthians. He uses each one to encourage the other to do better than they would do if they did not have such a good example.

He told the Corinthians, "Look at what God is doing with the Macedonians." He told the Macedonians, "Look at what God is doing with the Corinthians." It worked, because they all had the same God.

We go to missions conferences and hear examples of what some people are doing, and it makes us want to sign up. That is what a good example will do.

Last year I was in a church in Alabama that runs 1,100 in Sunday school and had a $1 million Faith Promise commitment. You might be saying, "Yeah, but we're in a building program." Well, they just came out of a $20 million building program. When I was a pastor, our church averaged close to 1,000 and gave $500,000 a year to missions. Sometimes a good example helps. You have the same God these churches have, so just let God do something.

Second, not only can other churches be our example, but other givers can as well. The Bible talks about one particular giver who was rich, but for our sakes became poor — Jesus. There is a good example. Jesus looked down at us and said, "For their sakes, I'll reduce my wealth. I'm walking on gold, living in a mansion, worshipped by the angels, but I'll go to Earth, live in a fleshly body, become homeless without any place to lay my head." What an example!

How many of us are willing to live like Christ did? Our definition of poverty in America is not being able to pay insurance on your boat. Compared to Jesus, we do not know how to give at all. *"Thanks be unto God for his unspeakable gift"* (2 Corinthians 9:15). *"For God so loved the world, that he gave his only begotten Son, that whosoever believeth in him should not perish, but have everlasting life"* (John 3:16).

We have two daughters and ten grandchildren in Africa. From a human standpoint, that is an unspeakable gift. Some of you who have missionaries in your family know the pain that you feel at the airport. I do not know how many times I stood and watched a giant airplane carry my loved ones out of my life.

I was in Boston recently as our youngest daughter's family was leaving to go back to Africa. We were all crying, and I was leading the pack. My granddaughter said, "Momma, what is Grandpa crying about? He gets to go home." Sometimes we might be more willing if we see what others are being called to contribute.

Third, it would help us is to see how much good our giving is going to do. I think it does more good to give than it does to keep it. It accomplishes this in several ways.

It does us good when we give. We say that we believe every word of the Bible. *"Give, and it shall be given unto you."* Is that in the Bible? Do we believe it? If we do, then we will have no problem with giving.

A missionary came through our town a while back. He was driving an old car that was in bad shape. I had just gotten a new Ford Crown Victoria; the church gave it to me. God led my wife and me to give that missionary our brand-new car. I am not saying this to brag; I am as greedy as anyone reading this book.

I gathered the deacons and said, "You all have been so kind to me over the years. Now you've given me this new car, and I love it, but God wants me to give it to that missionary. I won't do it if you don't want me to, but I know it's what God wants me to do."

They said, "Dr. Keen, you do what you want to. It's your car."

So I gave the missionary that car. Soon after that, I was given an Oldsmobile and a pickup truck. When I gave, it was given unto me.

Giving helps others. Look at 2 Corinthians 9:12. *"For the administration of this service not only supplieth the want of the saints, <u>but is abundant also by many thanksgivings unto God</u>."* When you give, it takes care of other people's needs.

It takes cares of the needs of our church. Philippians 4:19 says, *"But my God shall supply all your need according to his riches in glory by Christ Jesus."* I have met with people who have serious financial needs and told them, "God will take care of you." That is not what that verse is about. The book of Philippians is a prayer letter, written by a missionary to a supporting church. So when Paul talks in that verse about God supplying needs, he is talking about the needs of a church.

To put it in proper context, go back to verses 15-16. *"Now ye Philippians know also, that in the beginning of the gospel, when I departed from Macedonia, no church communicated with me as concerning giving and receiving, but ye only. For even in Thessalonica ye sent once and again unto my necessity."*

Tie the word "need" in one verse to the word "necessity" in verse 19. Because the church at Philippi took care of Paul's necessity, God took care of the church's need.

Your church might have a great need right now. But if you are not careful, you could let that need rob you of a supply. You might think that you cannot give because of some need you or your church has.

We were in building programs nearly all of the time I was pastoring in Milford, Ohio. Some of our largest giving experiences came during building programs. One time a man who mowed our grass for us (you wouldn't think he had anything) inherited $500,000 and gave $50,000 of that in the middle of a building program. God took care of our need because we took care of Paul's necessity.

Fourth, another thing that will make us willing is seeing the good effect that giving has on God. I am big on anything that has to do with God. I think we have humanized missions too much and taken out the divine element.

Philippians 4:18 says, *"But I have all, and abound: I am full, having received of Epaphroditus the things which were sent from you, an odour of a sweet smell, a sacrifice acceptable, wellpleasing to God."* When you respond in your Faith Promise giving, God is going to be well-pleased. It will be an acceptable sacrifice, an odor of a sweet smell. That is the effect that my giving has on my God. Why would I not want to give? It helps <u>me</u>, <u>others</u>, <u>my church</u> and <u>my God</u>; *"... and your zeal hath provoked very many"* (2 Corinthians 9:2). If that does not make you willing, you might need to head for the altar.

When you make your Faith Promise commitment, remember that it is an act of grace. *"See that ye abound in this grace also."* Grace, in the Bible, is often defined with the word "enabling." So read it this way: "See that ye abound in this enabling also."

Who is going to be behind the success of your giving? God is. He will enable you to give what He wants you to give. We do not know how He is going to do it. Who could have imagined that little boy, when he left his house with five loaves and two fishes, would be the only one in the crowd who brought food?

We had a lot of covered-dish dinners at church when I was pastor, and my wife always worried to death that there would not be enough food. If she had just read John 6, she would have been all right. The little boy came to the picnic, and God enabled him to have enough food for the need. I do not know how God will enable you to give, but if He leads you to do it, He will enable you to perform it.

A lady came to me once and asked, "Brother Keen, will you go see my husband?" To be honest, I did not want to go see him; he was an ex-convict from the Ohio State Penitentiary. He was a drunk and a wife-beater. He was mean, but she asked me to go, and I went.

I knocked on the door of their house. No one came to the door, but a voice said, "Come in." The lady's husband was in the house alone.

I said, "I'm your wife's pastor. She is burdened about your soul. You're not living right. Don't you think it's about time you got saved?"

He said, "Yeah, preacher. It's time I got saved."

We knelt in front of their old couch with broken springs and I led him to Christ. He became one of our bus drivers and a good friend to me.

A while after that, his wife called my wife and asked if they could have lunch together. They went to a restaurant and had their food and fellowship. When the bill came, the lady told my wife, "If you don't mind, I'll buy our lunch."

My wife, knowing their situation, said, "My husband and I planned to buy your lunch."

"But you don't understand. Before my husband got saved, we never paid our bills; he drank it up. Now he comes home every Friday and gives me the paycheck." She pulled the paycheck out of her purse. "Will you let me buy lunch?"

I do not know how God will get yours to you. I do know that He is an enabler, because it is by His grace, and He will give you what you need to do your part. Moses needed enough food to feed more than a million people twice a day for 40 years. What did he get? He got as much as his assignment required.

God has assigned you a part in reaching more than six billion people. How much do you think He will make available to you? As much as you need for your assignment. Why do we not, in Jesus' name, just allow God to push us out of our comfort zone — to get started if we have not started, or to grow if we have started? Let Him touch our going, our giving, and our praying.

ON PREACHING

"For unto us was the gospel preached, as well as unto them: but the word preached did not profit them, not being mixed with faith in them that heard it."

Hebrews 4:2

In the first half of verse 2, the apostle Paul is talking about two crowds that heard the same gospel (*"us"* and *"them"*). The remainder of the verse demonstrates that one crowd got nothing out of it (*"did not profit them"*) and then tells why they did not profit (*"not being mixed with faith in them that heard it"*).

How many times, I wonder, have we heard preaching that did not profit us? Now I am a preacher, so I am not trying to excuse preachers from sometimes being responsible for profitless sermons. Nor am I willing to let us take all the responsibility and shoulder all the guilt when a sermon is profitless to the attendee. Hearers have a responsibility to hear. Thirteen times in the New Testament Jesus said, *"He that hath ears to hear, let him hear."* Paul said that sometimes we hear preaching that does not profit us and the reason lies at the feet of the one doing the hearing (*"not being mixed with faith in them that heard"*) during that sermon.

Too often, if we are not careful, we gauge the value of the sermon on the quality of the oratory or the quality of the presentation — whether it is humorous, or short, or loud, or intellectual. We look at it based upon what we like, and whether the preacher is saying it in a way we enjoy. If we do not enjoy it, we may think that he is not a good preacher or his sermon is not good preaching.

Paul said that some people did not profit from preaching, not because of the inability of the preacher, but because they did not mix what they heard with faith. So as far as the problem of not being blessed by preaching, he laid that responsibility in the lap of the hearer, not the preacher. Now I have heard some preaching and done some preaching that was not very profitable. But right now I want to help you have more faith in preaching than what you have. One way to increase your faith in preaching is to know the value of it.

Preaching is God's powerful and designed way of publishing and propagating the Christian faith. Not singing, not drama, not chanting, not clapping, but preaching. That is God's choice; *"it pleased God by the foolishness of preaching to save them that believe"* (I Corinthians 1:21).

Some of those other things are of great benefit, but the first choice is preaching. Keep that in mind. The most important time of a church service is the preaching time. I did not say that; God did.

There is a difference between a prophet or apostle and a preacher. A prophet/apostle **tells** new truth. You have never heard a prophet or apostle, but you have heard of them. You have read in the Bible about what they said, but you have never actually heard one. A prophet was a man who came on the scene and gave the world new truth from God. The same thing can be said for the New Testament apostle. We are neither prophets nor apostles, but we are God-called preachers.

A preacher faithfully repeats the truth given by prophets and apostles. As preachers we are only parroting, expanding upon, and explaining what the prophets and apostles have delivered to us.

The revivalist James Stewart said, "The aim of preaching is to quicken the conscience by the **holiness** of God, to feed the mind with the **truth** of God, to purge the imagination to the **beauty** of God, to open the heart to the **love** of God, and to devote the will to the **purpose** of God." That is what preaching is to do.

Cotton Mather, another preacher in New England hundreds of years ago, said, "The grand design of the Christian preacher is to restore the throne rights and dominion of God to the soul of man." He said that the world is starving for a view of the greatness of God, and the greatest way we can show God is through preaching.

I. The church is in need of a vision of the greatness of God, and that is the first goal of preaching. If the preacher has completed his assignment when you leave a church service, there ought to be something about God that has been promoted in your heart. The job of the preacher is not to give you a pep talk or a psychological lesson on life. There are others who can do that, and you need that occasionally. If a preacher does not proclaim the greatness of God weekly to his people, who is going to do it?

So we need to know the value of preaching and have faith in it. It is the single most powerful communication tool from God to us in the world today.

II. Now I know that many of you have heard as many sermons as I have. But there are some things that you need to think about when you hear a sermon.

A. <u>The text from which the preacher is preaching is God's Word.</u>

1. It has a value unlike any other book, passage or writing. The text is divine in its origin, its nature and its authority. If the preacher is preaching from the Bible, then we are listening to the inspired (God-breathed) Word of God. That gives it value.

2. The text that the preacher is using is part of God's initiative to reveal Himself to me. The Bible is not an authorized biography but is autobiographical. It is about God and authored by God. When I read the Bible, I am studying an inspired text that God gave to me so that He could reveal Himself. When I hear it preached I need to listen to it as an inspired autobiographical effort.

3. This text is so important that God preserved it from when it was first penned until now. We have the preserved, inspired Word of God. It was written 2,000–4,000 years ago. Why did He preserve it? Because it still has value today. God did not preserve everything He wrote. Jesus wrote in the sand; that was not preserved. The Bible says that the world could not contain everything that has been written or could be written about Christ. *"And there are also many other things which Jesus did, the which, if they should be written every one, I suppose that*

even the world itself could not contain the books that should be written" (John 21:25). But He did preserve certain passages for us to use today, because they are valuable to us.

4. I listen to a text used by a preacher in a sermon because the providence of God allowed me to be exposed to it. Think about that. God permitted you to be in church last Sunday to hear what the preacher had to say from God's Word. That should make you wonder what God might want to say to you through that text. These wonderful attributes of God's Word are being pointed out to you to help build your faith, because preaching will not be profitable to you unless it is integrated with your faith. God arranged it so you would be exposed to this particular text.

5. Regardless of how frequently you have heard a particular text, you still do not know a great deal about it. A lot of people think that since they have heard a verse a couple of times in a sermon, there is nothing else in that verse for them. I do not care how much preaching you have heard on a specific passage, there are still volumes that you do not know about it. Are we so proud to think that, with our finite minds, we can delve into the depths of the mind of God through a couple of thirty-minute sermons from one text? Take a good look in the Bible and see how often Jesus repeated Himself. There are four gospels. Deuteronomy is essentially a review of the first four books of the Bible. So when you hear a text, the last thing you should say is, "Well, I heard that preached on when I was a kid. I know all about that. I guess I'll just sit here and be bored." You do not understand all there is to know. *"Wherefore I will not be negligent to put you always in remembrance of these things, though ye know them, and be established in the present truth"* (2 Peter 1:12).

It also does not hurt to listen again to something which you may have already heard. I have some favorite meals that my wife cooks. I would be a sorry husband if I said to her, "I'm not eating mashed potatoes again. We had them a few years ago." I like to eat some of her special dishes over and over. Her roast beef is so good that it will make your tongue beat your brains out. We should treat the spiritual food we get from the Word of God the same way we look at our favorite physical food.

The feeding of the 5,000 is recorded in each of the gospels. Why would God tell about the same miracle four times? Obviously, He thought there was valuable truth for us to glean from it each time. We can always learn more from repetitive exposure to His Word.

B. <u>There are two things you, as a listener, have a right to expect from the preacher as he deals with the text from God's Word.</u>

1. First, he (the preacher) should be faithful to that text and let the Author (God) say what He desires to say. We as preachers should not try to use a passage just to serve our own personal needs.

I think you have a right to go to church, hear the Bible preached and know that he is preaching what the Bible says. I've heard some sermons where the preacher did not even need a Bible. I have heard preachers who did not even open a Bible. You need a pastor who, when he opens to a certain text, will preach what that text says (whether you like it or not).

I need to preach on sin, and I need to have a good spirit when I do. People have a love-hate relationship with sermons on sin. They want to hear it and know they need it, but they also do not want to hear it. God will give people the strength to transform their lives if they are Biblically challenged.

Homosexuality, same-sex marriage, pornography, abortion — these are all things we have to deal with, because the Bible addresses them. But we need to have a good spirit when we deal with them. You need to believe that when you come into your church on Sunday, you are going to hear the Bible preached truthfully.

2. Second, you have a right to expect the preacher to make

an application of his text to the world in which we live. Now there is a difference between application and interpretation. In the Bible there is only one true interpretation of any particular verse, but there are many applications. It is necessary to make an application when preaching because those verses were written in a world in which you and I did not live. If you cannot take a verse and bring it to my circumstances and apply it where I live, of what benefit is it to me?

Preachers are not historians. They are supposed to take what was written way back when and bring it here to us. For instance, what good is it to have a story about Jesus calming the angry waves on the Sea of Galilee if you do not live close to a sea? Will you ever get in a storm like that? Probably not. That story lets us know that He can calm the storms of our lives, and we all have those. Sometimes they are ferocious. You need to know that just like He did in that boat on the sea, He can get in your boat and still your storm. John Stott's theology would not be that of mine, but his definition of preaching is unsurpassed. In his book "Between Two Worlds," he defines preaching as a bridge connecting two worlds — the Bible world of several thousand years ago and our present world of today. This brings the truths of the past to the present by applying the ancient precepts to contemporary experiences.

What value is there in knowing that Jesus fed 5,000 at one time? Will you ever have to accomplish that? No, but we can apply that story today and know that our God is powerful enough to take care of our needs, no matter how large and out of proportion to your supply they may be. When Jesus forgave the woman at the well who had five husbands, and the thief on the cross, He was showing us that He can forgive us also. You need to know when you hear preaching that you can apply it to your personal everyday life.

3. <u>So you have a right to expect a number of things from a preacher. What can that preacher expect from you?</u>

1. He has a right to expect you to anticipate that God will be speaking to you through the text from which he is preaching. Whenever you sit in a church and hear a message, you should sit there knowing that God will speak to you. Say with Samuel, *"Speak, Lord; for thy servant heareth."* Think about that. If you were in a church service and knew that the president of the United States would be coming through the door at some point during the sermon, you would probably be sitting up straight and paying attention. You would arrive looking for a good seat. How would it affect our congregation if we came every week thinking about how we were about to hear from God? It would change our attitudes. "Straighten up, kids. Pay attention. We're about to hear from God."

When we expect to hear God speak to us from His Word through His man, it changes our minds, our desires, our willingness to respond — everything. We should put a sign out in front of the church that says, "Come hear God this week." God said He would speak to us through His Word, and I am expecting Him to do it. If He does not, it cannot be His fault. It would be my fault because I did not mix faith with His Word that was preached to me.

Think about a time you went to hear a famous preacher. God spoke to you, didn't He? It was because you had faith and expected Him to do so. You said, "I'm going to hear from God when I go hear Brother So-And-So." God honored your faith. You went away thinking, "Boy, God really moved tonight." He moved because you mixed faith with the preaching of His Word.

Do you want to be a blessing to your pastor? Come this Sunday expecting God to speak. When you mix your faith with your pastor's preaching, God will honor your faith.

2. The preacher also has a right to expect you to respond to the text being preached. That does not mean that you come to the altar in every service (though I suspect most of us do not come

forward too much but too little). If God does not speak and make something happen in your heart, what good is it? All it has done is keep you indoors for an hour. But if we believe that the Bible is the inspired Word of God, and the man of God presents it, and God speaks, He is going to call upon you to make some type of decision. It may be a decision you make right there in the pew.

There are many ways to respond to the message. If someone preaches about <u>God</u>, your response may be worship. If the sermon is about <u>sin</u>, your response may be confession. If Jesus is preached, the response could be seeing the <u>unsaved come</u> to Him. If the preaching is about promises, maybe we should start <u>inheriting</u> some of them. If it is the commandments, we might want to decide to <u>keep</u> them. If the preaching is about the world, it might make us <u>missionary-minded</u>. If it is about the future, it could give us <u>hope</u> regarding where some of our friends and family members are and the fact that we will see them again.

Every time you hear a preacher, it can and should be profitable to you. The requirement is your faith. *"For unto us was the gospel preached, as well as unto them: but the word did not profit them, not being mixed with faith in them that heard it"* (Hebrews 4:2).

WHAT I WISH I HAD KNOWN

"Therefore seeing we have this ministry, as we have received mercy, we faint not; But have renounced the hidden things of dishonesty, not walking in craftiness, nor handling the word of God deceitfully; but by manifestation of the truth commending ourselves to every man's conscience in the sight of God. But if our gospel be hid, it is hid to them that are lost: In whom the god of this world hath blinded the minds of them which believe not, lest the light of the glorious gospel of Christ, who is the image of God, should shine unto them. For we preach not ourselves, but Christ Jesus the Lord; and ourselves your servants for Jesus' sake."

2 Corinthians 4:1-5

I was saved the second Sunday of October in 1958 in Akron, Ohio, under the ministry of Dr. Dallas Billington. I got saved just to miss Hell (knowing if there was one I deserved to go there). That was the extent of my vision. On that eventful day in the fall of 1958, Mary and I were young newlyweds. I had attended the church as a boy on a bus and knew they loved project people like we were.

After I got saved, the Lord started stirring in my heart to teach Sunday school, so my wife and I started teaching seven-year-old girls. Then the Lord planted a desire in my heart to go to Bible college. Now I did not do well in high school. I attended Greensburg High School and out of a class of 52, I had the lowest grade point average in my graduating class in 1957. So I told the Lord, "I don't think that's for me. You'd better find something else for me to do."

I ended up attending Midwestern Baptist College in Pontiac, Michigan, where Dr. Tom Malone was the president. Upon graduating in 1964, I accepted the pastorate of First Baptist Church of Milford, Ohio, where we spent the next thirty-five years pastoring that church. It has now been more than forty years in the ministry, preaching an average of one sermon a day.

Looking back over my ministry, there are some things I wish I had known as I began in 1964.

<u>I. I wish I had known that a relationship **with** God was more important than results **for** God.</u>

When I graduated from Bible college, I was tremendously goal-oriented. I was very proactive, very focused. I did all I could to cause the ministry that God had given me to grow.

I was called to a little church in southern Ohio, in the Cincinnati suburb of Milford, when I was 24 years old. I thought I must have been a great preacher because they had called me to be their pastor. I found out later that the church had fallen on hard times and though they were few in number, they were good people who were tired of fighting and wanted to do something for God. When I got there, I found out why I had gotten the church — no one else wanted it. None of the pastors in the area would allow their preacher boys to candidate there.

I did all I could to make that church grow, because I thought that satisfaction in Christianity was found in size. I thought it was found in success as the world deems it. So I went to all of the conferences that I could find on church growth. I already knew that sin did not satisfy the sinner, but I found out quickly that <u>service does not satisfy the saint</u>.

He is our satisfaction. *"Sir, we would see Jesus."* He is what satisfies the Christian. "Show us the Father, and it suffices us."

No one had made it clear to me when I finished school, so I thought satisfaction in the Christian life came from size, success and growth. But then I started observing those around me.

I watched Sunday school teachers who would teach for a couple of years and then drop out. I thought to myself, "If it's so satisfying, why are they quitting?"

I watched preachers go from church to church. The U.S. Postal Service reports that pastors change addresses every 18 months. I am not sure we change churches that often, but we do move around the community that often. If a pastor is not careful, about every five years or so he runs out of sermons and has to find another church.

I started asking myself, if service is supposed to be satisfying, why are all of those preachers changing churches so often or, even worse, quitting the ministry? Why do missionaries go to the field for one term and 50 percent never go back for another term? Why do laymen, out of a lifetime of church attendance, have an average of two years in local church service? Maybe there is not as much satisfaction in service and ministry as I once thought.

I started reading the Bible. I had read it before, but I had never seen it like this. I saw some of God's greatest servants having great dissatisfaction while they served.

I saw MOSES, the greatest servant of God in human history. He performed ten miracles in Egypt; I have not performed even one. He divided the Red Sea. He fed a million people two meals every day for forty years. He brought water from a rock. He really had a good thing going. Moses put up the first building in God's work, the tabernacle. From Mt. Sinai he became the first Bible publisher.

Do you know what he said in Exodus 33:18? *"Shew me thy glory."* He was saying, "Thank God for this wonderful ministry, but without You there is something lacking."

Who cares if you can divide seas, do miracles, print Bibles, build buildings, and feed millions if you are not fellowshipping with the God of Heaven? In that verse, Moses simply stated his dissatisfaction.

Then I started thinking about DAVID. He was the great lion, bear and giant killer. While still in his teens he was a national hero, having killed his ten thousands while the king only killed his thousands. He was a great musician and song writer. David was a king and a friend to the prophet Samuel. He wrote most of the biggest book in the Bible. What a man of service and great works.

Yet in Psalm 42:1, he said, *"As the hart panteth after the water brooks, so panteth my soul after thee, O God."*

What does that mean? It means, "Thank God I can kill bears and lions; thank God I can kill Goliath; thank God I can write psalms; thank God I have a place of authority. But there is still something missing. It is a deep, abiding relationship with God." Thank God for the ministry He may give you, but you will also be missing something if you do not know to seek God.

Think about the apostle PAUL. He had the greatest conversion experience of anyone of whom I have ever read or heard. He saw the Lord brighter than the noonday sun, and another time he was caught up to the third heaven. He had a worldwide ministry and was a great church planter. He wrote thirteen or fourteen books in the New Testament, depending upon your theology. (Do you know anyone else who has had fourteen best-sellers for 2,000 years?) There is some discussion about whether he wrote the book of Hebrews (someone said that John R. Rice wrote it, but I do not think that is true). He was undoubtedly Christianity's best product and the church's greatest theologian.

But he said in Philippians 3:8, *"Yea doubtless, and I count all things but loss for the excellency of the knowledge of Christ Jesus my Lord: for whom I have suffered the loss of all things, and do count them but dung, that I may win Christ."* Nothing was of any value to Paul in light of knowing Him. *"That I may know him ..."*

I wish I had known (back when I was 24 years old and fresh out of Bible college, wondering if God would ever do anything with me) how a relationship with God is more important than results.

I am not against results, but I want them to come out of my relationship with Him, and so should you. Go where He is — in the prayer closet, in the Bible, in Christian fellowship, and in the fellowship of suffering. Get to know Him. *"... Mary hath chosen that good part ..."*

He is in the closet. Find a place every day where you shut out the world and everyone else in it and get alone with God.

He is in the Book. Get in the Word of God every day.

He is in the congregation of the righteous. Make certain that you are regularly attending the house of the Lord.

II. I wish I had known that no man's ministry is a **model** for another man's ministry.

You can learn from others, but you cannot always be what they are. Dr. Tom Malone used to say, "If God wanted two John the Baptists, He would have made him twins."

God does not always want me to do what another man did or is doing. When I realize that, it might keep me from being jealous or critical. If I try to do what someone else did and I cannot succeed, I might start trying to tear him down, be jealous, or attempt the work of God in the flesh. *"For we dare not make ourselves of the number, or compare ourselves with some that commend themselves: but they measuring themselves by themselves, and comparing themselves among themselves, are not wise. But we will not boast of things without our measure, but according to the measure of the rule which God hath distributed to us, a measure to reach even unto you. For we stretch not ourselves beyond our measure, as though we reached not unto you: for we are come as far as to you also in preaching the gospel of Christ"* (2 Corinthians 10:12-14).

I have learned that God does not want all of us doing the same thing. How many of the Bible characters divided a Red Sea? In fact, not only does He not always want us to do what others have done, He does not always intend to do some things in my life He has done previously. He does things in my life He probably will not be doing again. How many children did Mary have through the virgin birth? I have learned, to my shame, that there are some things I have tried for God that He never wanted in the first place.

If we are not careful, we will try to mimic roles that we respect, but we end up being something God does not want us to be. How many people did God want to walk on water? Do not try that; it was for someone else. How many did He want to ride in a fiery chariot, build an ark, give birth to a son at 90 years of age, or have a Son with no human father? God may not want you to do what someone else did, but He has something special for you. Find out what it is and do it.

I do not even think Jesus' ministry is an exact model for us. Many charismatics are out there trying to mimic Jesus. (His character is a model.) I do not think He wants me raising the dead, feeding 5,000 or walking on water. He has something special He wants me to do.

More than thirty years ago I met a man named Don Frazier. He was a bit different. He did not know anything except that the world needs the Bible. He burdened my heart about printing the Bible and we founded Bearing Precious Seed. I did not go out and tell everyone to print Bibles, because I did not think everyone was supposed to do it. That was what God wanted us to do.

Years later I became burdened about our church's buildings, and we built $10.5 million worth of buildings debt-free. I have had many preachers come to me and say, "Why don't you write a book about building debt-free?" I never did that because I am not sure everyone else should do it the way we did it, or that I should do it the way you did it, or that I should do it again. Anyway, that is the wrong question; it is not **how** to build debt-free, but **why** build debt-free.

You know how we are. If I had lived in Peter's day, when I saw him walk on water I probably would have said, "Where did you learn that? Where is the conference that teaches that ministry approach?" Everyone is not supposed to do it the same way. I wish I had known this when I was a young preacher so I would not have had to learn it over the years.

III. I wish I had known the difference between a **bunch** and a **body**.

After about twenty-five years in the ministry, I realized what a church is. It is not necessarily a bunch of people in a building on a tax-free piece of property. For a long time, I thought the goal was just to win 'em, wet 'em and work 'em. But the Lord Jesus Christ meant for us to have a church.

A church is a body of people who have been born again and baptized, bonding together in a common goal of world evangelism, ministering to each other in the power of the Spirit of God through the authority of the Lord Jesus Christ. (This is more a practical description than a theological one.) It is not just a bunch of people gathering to hear some great preacher, sing some great songs, put their silver in the pot and then go home. That is not a body.

There is a difference in church growth and the church swell; both are involved in size increase. The body grows because it is healthy. The bunch is more swollen because of infection. Healthy growth is slow; body swelling is rapid. (The exception to this comparison is when the church body is in revival.)

While pastoring I also realized that I was not the only person on the property on Sunday morning with something of value to say. With that in mind I started twenty-three adult Bible classes. There were some wonderful men and women who walked with God, who loved the church and souls of men, and who could and would minister His Word.

I met with those lay teachers on Thursday nights and taught them the lesson. Then they went and taught it Sunday morning with their own illustrations and applications, out of their known experiences. Our adult attendance doubled in five years as they ministered to each other.

I took down all of the signs that referred to reserved parking spaces for the church staff. I told the staff, "If you want a good parking space, come early."

I also took the staff off the platform. On Sunday morning we looked like a Fortune 500 company with the CEO and executive staff sitting up there, all dressed alike in white shirts, black suits and ties, black socks, etc. I am not saying this is for every church, but I wanted to become one of the regular people. I wanted them to know they were of value.

I was raised in Akron, Ohio, in a project area called Hillwood Homes. (Cleveland Cavaliers basketball star LeBron James was raised in the same project years later.) We were poor folks. My dad was from West Virginia and had quit school in the 10th grade to go to work. He moved us to Akron so he could accept a job at General Tire & Rubber.

The county nurse came through every spring to check on us

and see how we had fared during the winter. She looked down my throat and said to my dad, "You need to have that boy's tonsils out."

"Why?" said Dad. "Are they infected?"

"No. But he doesn't need them."

"Maybe you're educated and I'm not," he answered. "But God didn't give that boy any spare parts. If he's got 'em, he needs 'em."

What he was saying was that every member of my body has a function. If you are a member of a church, you have a function. You are very valuable. We are not all noses, all ears, all eyes, or all mouths, but each of us is to minister to the others like the different parts of the body minister to the rest of the body. You have something you can do for the **good** of your church and the **glory** of your God. So let us have a church that is a **body** and not just a **bunch**.

IV. I wish I had known the difference between **fruit** and **results**.

I am afraid I did more result producing than fruit bearing. I am not even sure I always know how to tell the difference.

The difference must lie somewhere between training people to ask the right questions in order to get a desired response and trusting the Holy Spirit to produce conviction, confession and repentance. I am sure my motives were not always right, but I am just as sure my motives do not affect the power of the gospel (though they might affect my rewards at the Bema).

Paul said in Philippians 1:15-18, *"Some indeed preach Christ even of envy and strife; and some also of good will: The one preach Christ of contention, not sincerely, supposing to add affliction to my bonds: But the other of love, knowing that I am set for the defence of the gospel. What then? notwithstanding, every way, whether in pretence, or in truth, Christ is preached; and I therein do rejoice, yea, and will rejoice."* Some preached Jesus out of good motives and some out of bad. Nevertheless they rejoiced either way in the fact that He was being preached.

I also learned I was a bad fruit inspector. I was not always able to tell which was fruit that would remain. I only know there is a difference between fruit and results. Results are cause by a transfer of information; fruit is caused by a transfer of life.

I trust that you not take as many years to learn these truths as I have.

DEFINITIONS

A people group is a large number of individuals who have a close relationship and sympathies with (affinity for) one another because of a common origin, such as tribe, race, ethnicity, as well as a common culture that would include language, religion, occupation, etc. It is the largest group of people through whom the Gospel can flow without meeting cultural barriers. A people group is considered **unreached** when there is no indigenous community of believing Christians with adequate numbers and resources to evangelize this people group without outside assistance. There are over 6,000 unreached people groups in our world.

The 10/40 Window is a rectangular geographical box, which stretches between the 10th and 40th parallels and from the west of Africa to Japan in the east. Within the 66 nations in the Window exist 97 percent of the 6,000 unreached people groups in the world (3.6 billion people). The majority of these groups do not have the Scriptures in their language or dialect.

TOP 100 UNREACHED PEOPLE GROUPS

PEOPLE	COUNTRY	POP.	Main Religion
Ansari	India	9,871,000	Islam
Arab, Algerian	Algeria	19,540,000	Islam
Arab, Iraqi	Iraq	15,845,000	Islam
Arab, Moroccan	Morocco	14,549,000	Islam
Arab, Saudi - Hijazi	Saudi Arabia	9,606,000	Islam
Arab, Saudi - Najdi	Saudi Arabia	8,131,000	Islam
Arab, Ta'izz-Adeni	Yemen	9,418,000	Islam
Arab, Tunisian	Tunisia	6,701,000	Islam
Azerbaijani, Azeri Turk	Iran	14,500,000	Islam
Azerbaijani, North	Azerbaijan	6,417,000	Islam
Badhai, Hindu	India	5,488,000	Hinduism
Bania	India	22,644,000	Hinduism
Bengali	Bangladesh	99,068,000	Islam
Bhoi, Hindu	India	5,429,000	Hinduism
Brahman	India	57,825,000	Hinduism
Burmese	Burma (Myanmar)	27,702,000	Buddhism
Dhobi, Hindu	India	11,286,000	Hinduism
Dominican, Mixed	Dominican Republic	6,178,000	Unknown
Fulani, Toroobe	Nigeria	6,272,000	Islam
Gadaria, Hindu	India	5,630,000	Hinduism
Gujar	India	5,862,000	Hinduism
Hakka	China	31,935,000	Non-Religious
Han Chinese, Xiang	China	36,785,000	Non-Religious
Hausa, Ajawa	Nigeria	24,226,000	Islam
Hui	China	10,890,000	Islam
Irani	Iran	23,630,000	Islam
Japanese	Japan	122,064,000	Buddhism
Jat	India	13,620,000	Hinduism
Jat, Sikh	India	11,453,000	Other/Small
Jawa Banyumasan	Indonesia	6,682,000	Islam
Jawa Mancanegari	Indonesia	18,830,000	Islam
Jawa Pesisir Lor	Indonesia	21,000,000	Islam
Kachhi, Hindu	India	5,167,000	Hinduism
Kahar	India	6,869,000	Hinduism
Kashmiri Muslim	India	5,888,000	Islam
Kayastha	India	7,134,000	Hinduism
Kazakh	Kazakhstan	8,663,000	Islam
Khmer	Cambodia	12,575,000	Buddhism
Koiri	India	6,665,000	Hinduism
Koli	India	11,211,000	Hinduism
Korean	Korea, North	22,605,000	Non-Religious
Kumhar	India	13,290,000	Hinduism
Kunbi	India	24,507,000	Hinduism
Kurd, Turkish	Turkey	5,678,000	Islam
Kurmanji, Northern Kurd	Turkey	6,387,000	Islam
Kurmi	India	15,368,000	Hinduism
Lingayat	India	9,095,000	Hinduism
Lodha	India	5,987,000	Hinduism
Lohar	India	8,110,000	Hinduism
Madiga	India	6,759,000	Hinduism

Source: Joshua Project (www.joshuaproject.net)

TOP 100 UNREACHED PEOPLE GROUPS

PEOPLE	COUNTRY	POP.	Main Religion
Madura	Indonesia	13,667,000	Islam
Mahar, Hindu	India	8,206,000	Hinduism
Mahishya	India	9,494,000	Hinduism
Mahratta	India	26,579,000	Hinduism
Mahratta Kunbi	India	6,449,000	Hinduism
Mala	India	5,214,000	Hinduism
Mali	India	8,497,000	Hinduism
Manchu	China	12,920,000	Non-Religious
Mappila	India	9,381,000	Islam
Minangkabau	Indonesia	8,200,000	Islam
Mongol	China	5,928,000	Buddhism
Mutrasi	India	4,739,000	Hinduism
Nai	India	10,297,000	Hinduism
Nair	India	6,778,000	Hinduism
Namasudra, Hindu	Bangladesh	5,335,000	Hinduism
Nau Buddh	India	7,171,000	Buddhism
Pasi, Hindu	India	6,653,000	Hinduism
Pathan, Southern	India	11,496,000	Islam
Pendalungan	Indonesia	6,580,000	Islam
Punjabi, Southern, Saraiki	Pakistan	15,370,000	Islam
Punjabi, Western	Pakistan	67,300,000	Islam
Pushtun, Southern, Afghani	Afghanistan	10,641,000	Islam
Pushtun, Southern, Afghani	Pakistan	12,296,000	Islam
Rajput	India	36,877,000	Hinduism
Rohingya	Bangladesh	14,279,000	Islam
Sanaani, Northern Yemeni	Yemen	8,916,000	Islam
Sayyid	India	7,027,000	Islam
Serb	Serbia & Montenegra	6,596,000	Non-Religious
Shaikh	India	71,045,000	Islam
Sindh	Pakistan	18,444,000	Islam
Sinhalese, Singhalese	Sri Lanka	13,203,000	Buddhism
Somali	Somalia	8,032,000	Islam
Sonar	India	6,584,000	Hinduism
Sunda	Indonesia	30,650,000	Islam
Tai, Northern	Thailand	6,187,000	Buddhism
Tai, Southern	Thailand	5,050,000	Buddhism
Tatar	Russia	5,965,000	Islam
Teli	India	16,152,000	Hinduism
Thai, Central	Thailand	18,232,000	Buddhism
Thai, Northeastern	Thailand	18,439,000	Buddhism
Tujia	China	7,500,000	Ethnic religions
Turk	Turkey	51,700,000	Islam
Urdu	Pakistan	11,989,000	Islam
Uyghur	China	9,222,000	Islam
Uzbek, Northern	Uzbekistan	20,500,000	Islam
Vakkaliga	India	6,659,000	Hinduism
Vanniyan	India	11,188,000	Hinduism
Viswakarma	India	7,644,000	Hinduism
Yadava	India	53,426,000	Hinduism
Zhuang, Northern	China	11,799,000	Ethnic religions

Source: Joshua Project (www.joshuaproject.net)

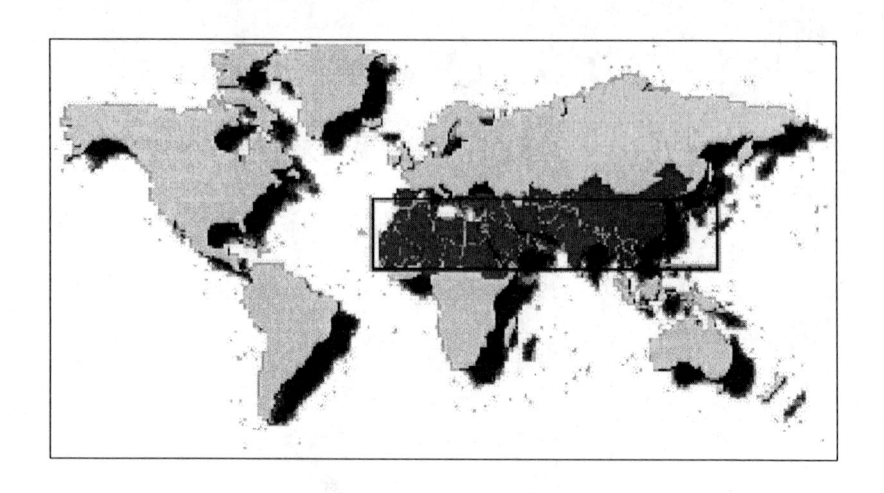

COUNTRIES IN THE 10/40 WINDOW

Afghanistan	Hong Kong	Pakistan
Algeria	India	Philippines
Armenia	Iran	Portugal
Azerbaijan	Iraq	Qatar
Bahrain	Israel	Saudi Arabia
Bangladesh	Japan	Senegal
Benin	Jordan	Somalia
Bhutan	Korea, North	Spain
Burkina Faso	Korea, South	Sudan
Cambodia	Kuwait	Syria
Chad	Laos	Taiwan
China	Lebanon	Tajikistan
Cyprus	Libya	Thailand
Djibouti	Macau	Tunisia
Egypt	Mali	Turkey
Ethiopia	Malta	Turkmenistan
Gambia	Mauritania	United Arab Republic
Gaza Strip	Morocco	Uzbekistan
Gibraltar	Myanmar	Vietnam
Greece	Nepal	West Bank
Guinea	Niger	Western Sahara
Guinea-Bissau	Nigeria	Yemen
	Oman	